Souper
Weight Loss
Secrets

Lillie Ross

Copyright 2003 by Lillie Ross Productions

All rights reserved.

The sale of this book is with the understanding that the author and publisher do not render medical or any other professional counseling. The reader is hereby notified that he or she should consult a medical doctor before applying the advice in this book... or before starting any exercise or weight loss plan.

ISBN 0-9719885-7-9

Second Edition

Published by:

**Lillie Ross Productions
105 Creekmore Road
Greenville MS 38701
USA**

Printed in the United States of America

Table of Contents

Dedication

Dedicated to my dear mother, who was the "original" Lillie Ross. To my older sister, Snookie, who was always proud of me... no matter what. Also, to my older sister Topsy, who if she were still alive, would hopefully read this book and for once in her life... be proud of her dratted "little" sister.

To my husband, Murry who is also my editor and insists that all my "I"s be dotted and all my "T"s be crossed... and without whom this book would be impossible.

Last... but far from "least..." my appreciation in spades to my **Daily Weight Loss Tips** subscribers who have contributed greatly to what you are about to read.

From every continent and almost every country on earth, you have told me what works best for you and allowed me to help your fellow readers with their weight loss problems.

Without you, this volume would be quite "skinny" indeed! With your contributions... a person can hardly keep from losing weight and keeping it off if he or she follows through on the easy common sense secrets they learn in this book.

Here's to slimming down and feeling great!

Lillie

Introduction

By: *Guy Coalter, Newspaper Features Writer*

Lillie Ross is truly a breath of fresh air on the diet scene. The first thing she tells you is, "never go hungry, never deprive yourself of a food you really want... and for heavens sake, don't even think about taking a diet pill!"

Likewise, Lillie advises against buying expensive diet food packaged by the big weight loss companies. She shows you how to quickly lose the weight you want to lose by eating all you want of tasty items you'll get at your local supermarket or produce stand. (Save yourself 90% or more!)

Lillie seems like your best friend giving you advice... and like a true friend... knows all about you and loves you anyway. She has helped hundreds of people lose thousands of pounds and she will now help you!

For 15 years, Lillie Ross served as a professional weight loss counselor with one of the most respected and well-known weight loss programs anywhere... a company whose name is a trusted household word across the globe.

Lillie's clients have paid hundreds of dollars each for her weight loss advice and counseling. Collectively... they have lost literally **tons** of weight!

For the past three years Lillie has written a weight loss advice column on the internet. She has thousands of subscribers worldwide from New York to New Zealand and Seattle to Singapore. Some have called her, the "Dear Abby" of weight loss due to the outstanding personal help she gives her readers in losing the pounds and inches they want to lose.

You've bought all the fad diets... You've tried all the "magic" pills. (You're darn fortunate they didn't kill you, my friend!)

Now, you're going to learn some "insider" secrets on not only losing weight naturally... but also how to keep it off... look better, feel better, as well as impress and absolutely amaze those around you! All this while eating all you want of supermarket bought and home prepared food every day!

You can contact Lillie by writing her c/o her publisher,

Lillie Ross, c/o
Lillie Ross Productions
105 Creekmore Rd
Greenville MS 38701

Or, you may email her at **Lillie Ross** (lillie@lillieross.com)

Lillie would certainly enjoy hearing from you about the weight you have been able to lose using her plans, tips, recipes and secrets.

Chapter One

Please Read This First

Here in short outline form is Lillie's Souper Plan for losing weight and keeping it off.

1. We give you a recipe for a delicious vegetable soup. People get the "short" version of this recipe free on the internet when they subscribe to Lillie's Daily Weight Loss Tips. In this book, we expand on that recipe considerably... especially in telling you how to customize it to your taste and use it in your extended weight loss plan.

    Some people complain they simply don't like the taste of the soup. That's understandable... but in this book, we're going to show you how to spice and jazz up this recipe to your own taste that you will love.

2. You should be able to find all the ingredients for your soup in your local super market and/or produce stand. You will then prepare this soup in your own kitchen.

3. Next, we give you a plan in which you eat all you want of your Souper Soup each day along with specified other foods for seven days... and seven days only. This is a quickie weight loss week to help you jump-start your weight loss efforts. Many people lose 9 to 17 pounds or more during this first week... some more, some less.

4. When you've completed the one-week Souper Soup regimen, you are ready to get back to eating almost anything you want. We help you fit your favorite foods into a balanced and healthy diet... while you keep off your initial weight loss and continue to lose even more if you so desire. We have material in the

book to help you plan that balanced and healthy diet from foods you like.

5. After the first week... when you're on the "eat what you want as long as it is a balanced diet" regimen... your Souper Soup is still going to play a very vital roll in your weight loss efforts.

    A. You should have a small bowl of Souper Soup before each meal. This will curb your appetite and help you to be satisfied eating less of your regular foods.
    B. You may also make a meal from Souper Soup... eat all of it you want as one of your three meals a day.

6. Last, but not least... You get "Lillie's Secrets" for losing weight and keeping it off. These are little tid bits you will find invaluable in your weight loss efforts. Many of them give you little-known, no-effort tricks of the trade to either burn more calories and lose weight... or curb your appetite and lose weight while you feel full, satisfied and full of energy.

Want To Get Paid To Lose Weight?

Yes, you can now get paid to lose weight. Lillie Ross Productions will pay you for good quality "before and after" pictures that show a dramatic difference in your over-weight self and your lean self. They do not have to be professional photos... but should be good quality.

Think about it before you start Lillie's Souper Weight Loss Plan... and then when you have both before and after photos, send an email to publicity@lillieross.com and someone will be in touch with you to make an offer for your pictures if they can use them.

Chapter Two

Souper Soup Weight-Loss Recipe

Our lawyers tell us that we must tell you: You should check with your doctor before starting any diet. You should never start any diet unless you are in good health. This publisher is not a health professional and is not to be construed as giving medical or professional advice in any shape, form or fashion.

Having said that... here is the easiest, quickest, and safest way we know to lose a batch of weight in a week!

Use the following recipe to make a pot of this amazing vegetable soup.

Makes about 18 - 1 cup servings

1 - 46 oz. can V8 juice
1 - 14.5 oz. can of diced tomatoes
6 medium stalks of celery (approx. 1 cup)
1/2 medium cabbage, red or green (approx. 6 cups)
1 medium onion (approx. 1 cup) (Lillie prefers the sweet onions such as Vidalia)
6 medium carrots (Or pre-sliced to equal 1 1/2 cups)
2 medium green peppers (approx. 2 cups) (red and/or yellow can also be used)
1 envelope of Lipton Beefy Onion Soup Mix
1 - 14 oz. can Swanson's Lower Sodium Beef Broth
1 beef bouillon cube or package
1 tsp. garlic powder
1 tsp. black pepper

Chop and dice veggies. Add all ingredients into a large stock pot. Add water if necessary to bring liquids to almost twice the depth of the veggies in the pot. Bring to a boil, and stir as needed. Cook on low heat for about 2 hours... or until all the veggies are soft.

Add other seasonings such as curry, parsley, or any other spices or herbs to suit your taste.

Nutrition Facts - all values are per 1-cup serving

Calories 50, Calories from fat 3, Total Fat 0.3g, saturated fat 0g, Cholesterol 0 mg, Sodium 472 mg, Total Carbohydrate 10.1g, Dietary Fiber 2.6 g, Protein 1.7g

You may substitute Low Sodium V8 Juice and the resulting Sodium will be 321mg instead of 476mg per serving.

Some values may vary slightly depending on products used.

You may safely keep prepared soup in your refrigerator for up to one week.

Start your diet in the morning and weigh before you eat anything.

Following are the foods you can eat each day of the 7 days of quick weight loss program.

Day 1 - Any fruits you want except bananas - plus all the Souper Soup you want.

Day 2 - All the veggies you want, baked potato with margarine for dinner - plus all the Souper Soup you want.

Day 3 - Combine day 1 and 2, but no potato - plus all the Souper Soup you want.

Day 4 - Up to six bananas, all the skim milk you want - plus all the Souper Soup you want.

Day 5 - 10 to 20 ounces of beef, chicken or fish, a small can of tomatoes, - plus all the Souper Soup you want.

Day 6 - All the beef, chicken or fish and vegetables you want - plus all the Souper Soup you want.

Day 7 - Up to a cup of brown rice at both lunch and dinner, up to 12 ounces of unsweetened fruit juices and all the non-starchy vegetables you want (no beans, potatoes, etc.) - plus all the Souper Soup you want.

In addition to the above, You should drink at least 6 to 8 glasses of water each day.

You may add vinegar, lemon, herbs, soy sauce, worcestershire, ketchup or mustard to your foods to suit your taste.

Beef, chicken or fish should be baked or grilled... **no fried foods**. Consider steaming your veggies. Walmart Stores stock a line of great little electric veggie steamers in the $19.95 to $49.95 range that work great for us.

(Sorry... but no bread, alcohol, or carbonated beverages are allowed during the 7 days... not even diet soda. If you drink coffee or tea, it should be decaf and no sugar is allowed... artificial sweetener only)

Many people on this regimen report excess gas. Consider keeping a supply of "Beno," "Gasx," or other gas relief product on hand while you're on this plan. A few people report feeling light- headed and/or weak.

You should NOT stay on this diet more than 7 days without at least a three or four week break... while eating a balanced diet.

You may, however, keep Souper Soup as **part** of your lunch and/or dinner menu every day for as long as you like. Slowly eating a bowl before your main course is healthy and tends to keep you from overeating. One of Lillie's Daily Weight Loss Tip readers reports he even has a cup of Souper Soup before breakfast each day!

Weigh and pat yourself on the back before going to bed on the evening of day 7.

We would appreciate hearing about the weight-loss results you obtain with this recipe. Please email me at: lillie@lillieross.com

Frequently Asked Questions and Answers

Q. This looks like the cabbage soup diet. Is it the same?
A. We have had scads of inquiries along the lines of, "Is this the old cabbage soup diet, Mercy Hospital Diet, Mayo Clinic Diet," and numerous other such questions.

The answer is **NO, NO, NO** and **NO!**

Although the ingredients may be similar... along with the foods you can eat each of the seven days... this is a **completely** different and original "quickie" weight loss recipe. It is definitely **NOT** a "cabbage" diet. You'll never know it contains cabbage when you taste it.

If there is any predominate taste... it is **TOMATO**. Call it "the tomato soup diet" if you like. We call it simply, the "Souper Soup Weight Loss Recipe!" Believe me... **It Works!!**

Q. "I don't like bananas. May I leave them out of the diet?"
A. Sorry, but each food in this diet serves a purpose. If you leave out, or cut down on any item... your results are likely to be less than desired.

Q. "I am allergic to tomatoes. May I substitute another vegetable for them?"
A. Unfortunately, No. Tomatoes are an important element of this weight loss recipe. Do **not** use this diet if you are allergic to any ingredient in the Souper Soup recipe.

Q. "I can't find V8 Juice in my country. May I use some other juice?"
A. V8 Juice is a blend of eight vegetable juices distributed in the U.S.A. by the Campbell Soup Company. Ask your

grocery supplier if they can obtain it for you. The primary element in V8 is tomato juice. You may mix your own substitute by adding a small amount of as many vegetable juices as you can obtain with tomato juice and seasoning it to your taste.

Q. I am vegetarian... what can I substitute for the meat called for in Souper Soup?
A. You may substitute soy products or high fiber foods such as beans and peas for protein in the plan.

Soy products, beans, peas etc. are great choices for anyone on a weight loss plan... vegetarian or otherwise. Just don't add fats when you are cooking the beans and peas. High fiber foods are low in calories. There are so many great soy products available now and the tastes have improved immensely over the years.

You can substitute vegetable stock for the beef stock and skim soy milk for the skim milk

Switch the beef or chicken for various soy protein products like bun-less tofu burgers and bun-less veggie-dogs. You may also add a small handful of almonds on each of the meat days."

Q. "Thanks to your soup recipe, I lost fourteen pounds in a week. I quickly gained much of it back, however. May I safely use the Souper Soup diet every fourth week to keep my weight off?"
A. Absolutely NOT. This would be an unhealthy situation. The Souper Soup diet is designed as a quickie weight loss program to lose a small amount of weight in a short period of time. Any such fast weight loss is usually a water loss and is gained back quickly unless you graduate to a structured, balanced-diet weight loss plan.

You could probably use the quickie week once again after a three or four week break... but I strongly recommend you find a plan that will give you a more balanced, regular diet. It is important to make changes in your eating habits that will serve you in the long haul. It is easy to get bored with eating the same thing day in and day out. You really should not ever feel deprived. It is important to be able to eat foods you **really** like from time to time without guilt.

To continue to lose weight and keep it off after your week of "quickie" weight loss on this Souper Soup recipe, you should by all means use a long-term, healthy, balanced-diet weight loss program.

Our recommendation is the easy solution outlined in this book. Using the methods recommended in Lillie's Secrets, you can eat all you want of almost any and all foods while you lose weight and keep it off! No pills, no drugs, no complicated calorie or "points" counting! Lillie's Plan is safe, healthy, and enjoyable!

Chapter Three

Adding Interest and Spice To Your Souper Soup

Making the Souper Soup recipe available to our Daily Weight Loss Tip readers on the internet during the last three years has produced hundreds of messages... comments, complaints, and yes... many ways to improve the soup. We have chosen the best of the improvements for you here.

Some of these tips can be used for enhancing the soup while you're on your seven day, "quickie" weight loss plan. Others are for using the soup as **part** of a balanced diet in your continuing weight loss efforts.

I have mentioned before that some of our readers have continued using the soup as an **addition** to their regular weight loss plan. In researching weight loss, I have found that people who add soup of almost any type to their diet tend to eat less total food.

The reason is that soup is so satisfying. Whether you eat it cold or hot, it can be a great way to start a meal.

Possibly, when you were a child your mother gave you a warm cup of soup when you got home from school. There was nothing that could warm your "innards" more. Now, the smell of soup cooking in the kitchen can possibly bring back that warm fuzzy feeling... memories of love, satisfaction, and a full tummy.

Miss Manners (American newspaper columnist Judith Martin) asks us, "Do you have a kinder, more adaptable friend in the food world than soup? Who soothes you when you are ill? Who refuses to leave you when you are impoverished and stretches its resources to give you a hearty sustenance and cheer?"

"Who warms you in the winter and cools you in the summer? Yet who also is capable of doing honor to your richest table and impressing your most demanding guests? ...Soup does its loyal best, no matter what undignified conditions are imposed upon it. You don't catch steak hanging around when you're poor and sick, do you?"

Seriously, soup (especially our Souper Soup recipe) can be a great **addition** to your meals. Eat it slowly and savor every delicious bite as it goes down. Don't forget, you can make the Souper Soup suit your particular taste by adding the spices and herbs that you like.

When going to a restaurant, order the cup of soup. See if it doesn't help with overeating! Choose soups such as vegetable and chicken with rice. (The servings are larger.)

Soups like broccoli with cheese and clam chowder are cream based and are higher in calories as well as smaller servings. Keep this in mind when ordering.

Dr. Henry Jordan, University of Pennsylvania, in a 10-week dieting study involving 10,000 subjects says, "Eating soup at the outset of a meal slows rapid eating and blunts appetite before excessive food is consumed-- therefore a soup-laden diet can change eating habits and lead to weight loss."

Here's a very interesting study from Johns Hopkins University. For two weeks, they gave 12 men... one of three first courses... tomato soup, Muenster cheese on crackers, or fresh fruit... all before a large lunch.

Although the dishes contained the same number of calories, the men eating the soup tended to eat fewer calories after sipping the soup, than the ones munching on fruit or cheese and crackers.

The researchers think the reason is that the soup takes up a larger volume of space in the stomach. They found also that cold, low sodium soup reduced their appetite just as well as the ones that were warm and had a higher salt content.

The soup also is a high carbohydrate food. It releases the chemical serotonin that contributes to a feeling of well-being. This also may be a factor in soup's ability to satisfy.

When choosing between soup and salad at large meals... choose the soup and make it a tomato based one. It's much less fattening than the mayo salad dressings and the cream type soups. Soup just keeps on being a winner in any weight loss program.

We don't have to tell you, of course, that we are partial to our Souper Soup for that purpose!

So many diet sources recommend using soup in your diet to satisfy that empty spot a lot of us have. We received a great testimonial from one of our readers named Ron.

Ron has had great success using our Souper Soup as an **addition** to his long-term weight loss plan.

Ron writes, "It has been almost a year since I had my first bowl of Souper Soup. To regress a little, I had started at 239 lbs. the end of Oct. 2000 and by May 1, 2001 I had gone down to 194 lbs. As I wrote to you at the time, I continued to have the soup each day and was really happy with the results, but now I just wanted to maintain the current weight actually to stay under 200 lbs.

As of today Oct. 1, 2001, I weigh 196. I continue to have the Souper Soup each morning for breakfast, I feel great and 1/2 the age I felt one year ago. I eat all things from pizza to frozen yogurt, steaks, ribs, burgers etc. but when I see a gain of 2 or 3 lbs. I go back on the veggies, chicken and fish until I take it off, which never takes more than a couple of days.

I credit this to the soup, I guess the fact it has all the vitamins and minerals a person needs and the only problem is some gas, which I feel is a small price to pay for the great health. I will be 69 next month and I feel better than I did at 45."

As I have said so many times, you need to find what works for **you** and stick with it. What works for some may not work for others. But adding soup to your program might just be the thing you need to keep you satisfied.

All weight loss programs are like most things in life. You only get out of it what you put into it. We all have different levels of losing weight... but being persistent in the plan is the only way to ultimately achieve your weight loss goal.

Sometimes a letter comes across my desk that just says it all... this one from Alicia.

"I just wanted to drop you a note on how much weight my husband and I lost. We have previously tried the Cabbage Soup Diet and failed miserably because we could not stand all that cabbage, but your soup was absolutely delicious!

We added cilantro and on our day that we ate only soup with veggies we put veggies in the soup to have some change. We also drank fruit juice. And I drank coffee with hazelnut creamer (just a little - 1 cup a day).

The results, I lost 10 pounds and my husband lost 20lbs by day 5! I was 160lbs at 5'4" tall and now 2 months later I am 140lbs. And still losing little by little. My husband is 5'10" and was 260lbs and now is 230. It really does work and it was not difficult to stay on this diet for the 4 major days after that it was a breeze.

Thank you and I have passed this diet on to others who actually saw me 20lbs ago and asked me how I did it. Also, I didn't work out ."

Thank you Alicia for sharing this great testimonial to Souper Soup.

One of our readers, Suzanne, shared her experience with us and I'll let her tell you her story. We had to "clip" it a little for brevity... but not a word, period, or comma, however, has been changed. It's Suzzanne's story!

"I found your recipe (Souper Soup) and was motivated to write you. (clip) I decided to try it as a "cleanse" more than anything, also to lose a few pounds, but mostly to "clean up my diet" which had gone off course this past year.

I lost 15 pounds, and I feel GREAT. I exercised (... clip) Mostly walking, running, and one long hike per week. That was 6 months ago, and I have not gained one pound back.

My secret?"

"First, the diet (Souper Soup) got me back on track. No more bread and starch all day long, no more junk food, less alcohol. (I still have wine with dinner, but way less of other stuff).

Secondly, I STILL make one batch of Souper Soup per week, every Sunday. I add stuff to it now, like carrots, can of corn, eggplant, red and yellow peppers, zucchini, spinach, leeks, bok choy, parsley, and other soup bases for flavor. I have this at LEAST once a day in some form.

I do eat other foods too, like a normal person, but obviously less. And VERY little "junk". I just don't want or crave sweets like before.

I have found that the soup, when made real thick, and with a lot of tomato products, is a great PASTA sauce! It is also a great base to add sausage, or other meat too, for a "chilli" like meal. We add beans then, garlic, and cooked tofu, or turkey sausage.

In another words, you can use it as a base for lots of dishes. I LIKE it, and I crave it sometimes if I've been away from my pot all day, or even if I leave home for the weekend. I miss my vegetables!

That's all I wanted to say. I just wanted to share my story.

By the way, when my parents use the diet, they lose about 8 to 10 pounds each, each time. But they cheat. I did not cheat, not even one tiny bit. And then they go back to their old ways of eating, so they gain it back.

I have 2 woman friends who did this too. One cheated and made substitutions, the other did not. The one only lost 4 pounds, the second woman lost 12. I know the diet works. It's the different personalities of people that do not!"

Thanks Suzanne!!

Another reader followed the Souper Soup Plan for the week and lost seven pounds. He liked the soup so well that he still has a bowl of it as one of his meals each day. (He also eats two balanced meals--- which makes this safe.)

He has now lost 25 pounds and has taken a significant number of points off his blood pressure reading. What **great** results.

Another advantage of using the soup as a meal is that it is also a good way to get your "Five-or-More Veggies" for the day.

If you use your Souper Soup for a meal each day, you might consider adding about 3 ounces of lean broiled or grilled chicken, ham, or beef.

This is not part of the Souper Soup quick weight loss plan. Use it in addition to your regular healthy (at least two) balanced meals each day--- after you're off the seven day Souper Soup regimen.

One of our readers, Teresa, has shared some great tips with us for using sugar free Jell-o during her week on the Souper Soup quick-loss jump-start. Teresa tells it better than I ever could:

Quote: "Sugar-free Jell-o has become my best friend on this diet!

I put grapes, orange slices, or pineapple chunks in my Jell-o on my fruit days.

My grandma gave me a recipe for veggie Jell-o salad with lime or lemon Jell-o, shredded cabbage, chopped green peppers, chopped carrots and a little bit of chopped onion. I love it. (Although it would be better with a little mayo.) I eat this on my vegetable days.

And for the banana days, the old favorite!! Orange Jell-o with bananas!! This is saving me and I thought other dieters with a sweet tooth may need a little helper too!"

Thanks Teresa! This is an excellent "helper."

Two of our readers came up with great recipes for shakes or "smoothies" using skim milk and bananas on the "Souper Soup Recipe."

Joyce said, "I put the bananas in the skim milk with a little crushed ice cubes in the blender and made a shake. It was really good and also filling."

Mary said, "On the 'banana and skim milk day,' I made a smoothie! It was so yummy I just had to share. I broke a banana into chunks and placed them in the blender. Then, I put in about 1 1/2 cups of skim milk. Then, I added artificial sweetener, a little vanilla extract, and about a cup of ice. Then turned on the blender until the concoction was smooth."

Shake or Smoothie... both are super yummy! Thanks ladies.

One of the most important things with any weight loss program is to be creative. And, I have received some very creative tips from you, my readers.

Skye likes very spicy things, so on the Souper Soup she did the following:

"Instead of regular V8 I used Picante V8. Instead of diced tomatoes I used Rotel tomatoes. Instead of onion soup mix I used taco seasoning."

Skye said, "I like my food REALLY spicy, and this REALLY was! You may only substitute some of the items if you don't want to make it really really spicy."

Sue lives in the warm climate of South Africa and here's what she did with the "Souper Soup."

"I've made a large volume of the soup and place most in the deep freeze. Makes a wonderful chilled drink several times a day - almost like having gazpacho!" :-)

Sounds like Sue may have put her soup through a food processor to eliminate the solids if she uses it for a drink? That's a "souper" idea!

Diane came up with this suggestion. "To vary the taste of the Souper Soup, I add basil or Chilli powder to the individual serving, (not the whole pot) depending on my mood. Keeps it from getting boring. These happen to be my favorite tastes. You can use whatever seasonings you like. Another thing that I do is freeze it in individual servings."

Another reader said, "Recently I made the Souper Soup just for lunch during the week when I wasn't on the diet. Well I found a good little recipe... if you add some crushed low-fat Tostitos' tortilla chips and some fat-free Kraft American Cheese slices to your soup, it taste just like Tortilla Soup! I even add some hot sauce sometimes. I think it's wonderful!"

You can be as imaginative as you want when adding spices to the "Souper Soup." Any of the V-8 veggie type drinks can be used for the base... the regular, low-sodium, or hot & spicy.

One of our readers, Brenda, had this suggestion, "When I make the "Souper Soup," I add several packages of Unflavored Gelatin (soaked in water per the directions) while the soup is hot. This makes the soup "gel" when it is cold, and it travels better to work -- less chance of it leaking from the container. The gelatin adds protein, only a few calories, and makes the soup more filling."

Another reader writes, "I am sprinkling a tablespoon of ground flaxseed on it. This is supposedly great for fighting cancer and heart attacks, as it contains a high amount of omega 3. It makes the soup a little sweeter. That's the only difference in taste."

If you use the Souper Soup part-time, as this reader does, you may not be able to eat it up quick enough. He said his wife makes enough for seven days, and freezes all but enough for about three days.

Or, maybe you could freeze the soup in individual servings and pop it in the microwave as needed. It will keep better that way.

When I think there is just no other way you can prepare our Souper Soup recipe, someone comes up with another great idea.

Tish has invested in a Vita-Mix 5000. Vita-Mix Corporation bills itself as "the manufacturer and purveyor of durable, high-performance blending and mixing equipment. Tish calls it an "investment in our health."

When she makes Souper Soup she cuts the recipe in half, (the container will only hold about six cups.)

Tish cooks the onion soup mix according to the instructions on the packet. Then, she uses all fresh, raw veggies with the V-8 juice. By not cooking her veggies she saves all the natural vitamins and minerals. A few veggies are saved to add at the end along with the V-8 juice and onion soup.

She kicks her speed up all the way for 4 minutes and adds any saved veggies, seeds, cores and/or peels for the last 30 seconds. Result... "a smooth steaming hot liquid with a bit of crunch from the seeds cores and peels." She also adds parsley, (stems and all) mushrooms, and a bit of red pepper (to speed up the metabolism.)

Tish tells us, "This is a really great way to get your required fiber, especially for people like me who don't like so many things like lettuce and some of the cereals and grains you mentioned because if you add it to a soup, you don't taste it..."

She says her Vita-Mix makes "WONDERFUL SOUPER SOUP." So, if you are fortunate enough to own one of these magical machines, you might give it a try.

One of our most frequently asked questions is about adding variety to the Souper Soup Program.

One way you may add some variety on the days you have fruit on the Souper Soup plan is to cook your fruit. Grapefruit broils beautifully... as well as sliced bananas. Baked apples are delicious. Bake them at 350 degrees until they become soft.

The warmth of cooked fruit will give you a new and different taste to enjoy and savor. (Besides making your home smell divine.) Mixing your fruit for a fruit salad is another winner.

Veggies can be flavored with so many herbs and spices. You are limited only by your imagination. Whether cooked or in a salad, make veggies reflect your own personal taste. Be creative. I bet you were before you started a weight loss plan!

Souper Soup can actually become an International Taste Sensation right in your own kitchen. All you have to do is add some of your favorite spices.

Add the spices of India, such as curry. Make it have an Oriental flavor with soy sauce. For a taste of Italy, use (one of my husband's favorite spices) oregano... or is that Greek? And for you folks that like a bit of the Cajun "**hot**," use the Spicy Hot V-8 juice plus a little hot sauce. For people who like the Tex-Mex flavor, add some chilli powder and jalapeno peppers.

(The onion soup called for in the soup recipe is for flavor and if it does not mix with some of these choices you may omit it.)

Judy shared another taste for the Souper Soup... Sweet and Sour. She wrote, "Amounts: I would start with a couple of tablespoons of sweetener and maybe a tablespoon of sour salt or 1/4 cup of lemon juice and then taste. Maybe a little more depending on how you like it. These amounts are guesses because I usually just pour some in."

And for those like me who didn't know... "Sour salt" is also known as "citric acid." It is found usually where Jewish or Eastern European foods/seasonings are sold. Sometimes I have also found it in the regular spice sections of the supermarket.

Thanks Judy for a great idea!

Here are more "souper" creative ideas on adding taste and interest to your Souper Soup when you are on it for your seven-day quickie weight loss. Our reader, Sunny, writes: "When I could have my beef, chicken or fish on day 5, I grilled a chicken breast on my George Foreman grill and then after putting some soup in the blender, I heated it and ladled it over the chicken. You see, by that point I was getting a little tired of the soup so this way, it tasted all new and exciting!"

Thanks Sunny! We tried it and the taste was fantastic.

One of the questions I am frequently asked is why you can't drink diet drinks while on the Souper Soup plan?

Most of these drinks are loaded with sodium to make them taste better. And as you know, sodium causes you to retain fluid. However, Royal Crown Company Inc. puts out Diet Rite drinks that have no sodium. Also they contain no aspartame, caffeine or calories!

Diet Rite has a cola and a white grape flavor that I find are very good. And... I see no reason why you can't drink them while you're on our Souper Soup quick weight loss week.

My readers are always coming up with great ways to make Souper Soup fit their tastes and Angela writes that she adds Old Bay Seasoning. One of our friends uses this seasoning in gumbos. He makes the best gumbo around. Thanks Angela.

Do you find it difficult to lose weight? The older we get, it seems the harder it is to take off weight and the easier it is to gain it back.

Some people are very discouraged when they only lose a few pounds. I hear this daily from the e-mails I receive.

I am all for visuals. If I can see it for myself, then I can believe it. If you have spent a week on our Souper Soup recipe and are discouraged because you only lost a few pounds... you might try the following.

Get out a pound or two of meat such as hamburger and give it a look. Or maybe four sticks of butter. This is a pretty good pile, isn't it!? And then, when you double or triple it... WOW!

Don't be discouraged. For every pound lost, you are one step closer to your goal.

Chapter Four

Now Let's Get Started Losing More Weight... and Keeping It Off!

The 7 Most Effective Weight Loss "Secrets" You Will Ever Read

Read and heed the following "secrets." They are only secrets if you don't know them... and most people don't. They are "tricks" and little-known items I've discovered over a lifetime of controlling my own weight... plus my years of experience as a professional weight loss counselor for one of the world's most respected commercial weight loss enterprises.

Use these secrets to "cut corners," curb your appetite, and lose all the weight you want without ever being hungry.

Two of the secrets you are about to learn are covered in books which have sold thousands of copies on the internet for $20.00 and $39.00 respectively. In this chapter, you are basically getting a "bonus" valued at $59.00 just for secrets 2 and 3 alone.

Use these seven secrets and you will not have any need to count calories... points... or "mathematics" in your daily diet.

OK... so you have completed your week of "quickie" weight loss with Souper Soup. If you followed the recipe and directions exactly, you probably lost somewhere between five and twenty pounds, depending on how much weight you had to lose when you started. Now you are going to learn how to keep it off with very little effort.

A few people for one reason or another do not lose any weight during the week on the Souper Soup recipe. Others "cheat" a little and lose less than they'd like.

This chapter also applies to you if possibly you didn't like the taste of Souper Soup and decided to drop the idea... or, if you found you are allergic to one of the main ingredients of the Souper Soup recipe and couldn't eat it. In this chapter you're still going to get your money's worth many times over... even if one of those problems apply to you and Souper Soup is not your cup of tea.

Whatever your circumstances, you are going to learn how to not only maintain any "quickie" weight loss you achieved... but also continue to lose one to two pounds or more each week until you reach your "target" weight.

"One or two pounds is not much," you say? Well, keep it up for a year and you will have lost 50 to 100 pounds! If that is not enough, you definitely should have asked your doctor for a plan before you started to read this book.

First of all, you have to realize there are basically only two ways to lose weight:
(1) Consume less calories than your daily activity burns... or
(2) Burn more calories from your daily activities or exercise than you consume in food.

As the ads for this book promise... you will be able to lose the weight you want to lose while eating all you want of most of your favorite foods, never getting hungry, and never taking any kind of diet pill. Some of these seven primary secrets are covered later in the book in daily secrets... but they are definitely important enough to repeat them here.

With this plan you will lose weight steadily with very little effort on your part. You will be eating a complete balanced diet and will not have any cravings. You will have a completely satisfied and full feeling after each and every meal... as well as between meals!

1. A simple activity to help you avoid the "triggers" that lead you to binge eating.

Keep a Journal

In this day and age of e-mailing, we forget about actually taking a pen in hand and writing. But, one thing recommended by so many to help with weight lose efforts is keeping a journal.

It doesn't matter whether you keep your daily journal on your computer, in a spiral or a loose-leaf notebook. You should attempt to make some entries in your journal every night before going to bed... or first thing next morning.

Weigh yourself on the same day each week, either without any clothes or while wearing the same clothes each time. Measure your chest or bust, waist and hips. Enter your weight and measurements into your journal.

It is important to weigh and measure each week at the same time in relation to your bath. In other words... do not weigh and measure one week before your shower and the next week after your shower.

Not only do the pros recommend keeping up with what foods you are eating, but also your activities. Probably the most important activities are those "triggers" that start you on that vicious cycle of "binge eating."

Usually these triggers are actually feelings such as anger, boredom, guilt, anxiety, etc. They can occur in happy times or not so happy times. But, taking pen in hand and writing... like they taught us in school to write a newspaper article... who, what, where, when, and why... can help you pinpoint those triggers.

Maybe every time you get angry at some one who has hurt your feelings, you reach for the cookies (like I used to do.) You will show them... right? I don't think so. :-)

Maybe it's after work. It's been a very frustrating day, and you head for the refrigerator.

Do some TV commercials and magazine ads send you into an eating frenzy?

Could the time of day set you off? Do you get home from work and immediately head for the refrigerator?

Could a certain smell (such as popcorn at a mall or theater) be your "undoing?"

Or, could an emotional situation be the reason for overeating?

All of these things needed to be documented. Doing this is a good way to determine our overeating patterns. Keeping a journal or diary of your eating "triggers" is a good way to solve those overeating problems.

Knowing the cause can definitely help with the cure

So, pick up that pen and write down those feelings. Refer to them when the same feelings occur again, and you will begin to break those bad old habits.

2. Here's How Your Plate Can Be Your Very Best Weight Loss Friend

Imagine your plate is divided in halves across the center... one of the halves is again divided in half. You then have a plate divided into two small divisions and one large one.

One weight loss plan sells you such a fancy divided plate for $30.00, but you can go to Walmart and get one for $2 or so. You may have to settle for a plate divided four ways... but that's OK too. Just consider two of those divisions as one in what you're about to learn.

Ideally, you should probably have two divided plates for this plan... an 8 inch plate for breakfast and lunch... and a

9 or 10 inch one for dinner. With a little common sense on portions, however, one 9 or 10 inch plate will suffice for all three of your meals.

While you are at Walmart, you will do well to invest another $19 - $49 and buy yourself a George Foreman Electric Grill. This little appliance is going to eliminate up to 90 percent of the fat in whatever meat you cook on it... while at the same time actually adding to the taste of your meat. Believe me, this grill is everything and more the ads say about it. I'd hate to know I had to live without mine!

Now let's talk about the food you are going to put in your divided plate. In general, you can eat almost anything you want as long as you divide it as described below.

One of the small divisions of your plate is for your protein, the other small division for your starches, and the large half division is for your fruits and vegetables.

Your protein can be any type animal product... eggs, lean portions of beef or pork...chicken (without the skin,) fish or seafood.

Starches in your other small division of your plate are rice, beans, potatoes, pasta, etc.

Fruits and vegetables... hey, the sky is the limit. Whatever you like and ALL you want. Pile that half division of your plate as high as you like with fruits and veggies.

The portion size of your protein should be about the size of a deck of cards... or the size of the palm of your hand. The thickness of the protein item should not more than one inch... or two inches if your protein is fish or sea food.

If you have eggs as your breakfast protein... either have two eggs (cooked any style you like, but using only a "spray" cooking oil) and one slice of bread or one egg and two slices of bread. Whole grain bread is definitely best. In fact... one slice of white bread is equal to two slices of whole grain bread!

Some type fish or sea food is your ideal lunch and/or dinner protein. With fish or seafood as your protein, it can be twice as thick as any other type meat you choose! Again... you will do well to use your George Foreman to cook your meat. If not... you should bake or broil it... NEVER fry it. When either baking or broiling... try to use some type of "elevated" grill in your cooking pan. This way, any fat that cooks out will fall to the bottom.

Your "all you can eat" fruit and vegetables can be any fruit or any non-starchy vegetable you can find available. By far the most healthful method of cooking your veggies... as well as some of your starches such as rice, is to steam them. Trusty Walmart again comes to the rescue with several low cost veggie steamers that will last for years.

You may season your veggies any way you like them as long as you do not use seasonings containing fat. A small amount of "I Can't Believe It's Not Butter" spray along with a dash of salt and pepper will beef-up the taste of your veggies considerably. Also consider oregano, lemon pepper or other spices you like.

Now... on a separate plate you may prepare yourself a delicious salad. You can pile this plate high with unlimited amounts of raw cucumbers, mushrooms, lettuce, cabbage, peppers, tomatoes, carrots, olives, etc.

You should NOT, however add nuts, croutons, bacon bits, seeds, etc. A very small amount of those is more fattening than all the rest of your salad together!

You may use any salad dressing you like... even the creamy high fat type... as long as you use one of Lillie's favorite secrets in applying it. That secret is to always put your dressing in a small container on the side. Then, before each bite of salad... dip your fork into the salad dressing. You get the full flavor and taste of your dressing without the high fat and calories!

You will do well to eat the salad, fruit and veggie portions of your meal first.

By now you're asking, "But, what about dessert? No problem! Eat a small slice of your favorite pie or a small helping of your favorite ice cream a few times a week.

Try not to deprive yourself of anything you ordinarily crave. Just try to limit your portion. Better yet is to try to satisfy your sweet tooth with a sweet apple, pineapple, etc.

3. "The Weight-Loss Miracle You've Been Waiting For! Cut 1,000 Calories A Day Without Dieting."

Could This Be Lillie's Best Secret Ever?

When attempting to lose weight, anything you can do to burn a few extra calories with very little if any effort is usually a winner.

We recently asked our staff to review all the tips we have published in the past three years... and choose the one they thought was the most impressive of all. They chose a tip we published almost three years ago. It told how to cut 1000 calories a day without exercise or dieting.

At one time or another, we all wish for a "magic pill" to help us lose weight. Wouldn't it be nice to just take one pill a day... eat all we want... and still lose all the weight we want to lose. Sorry to say, no such pill exists. But... a somewhat "magic **method of eating**" does exist that gives us almost those same results we are looking for in the pill!

About a year after we published our "magic" tip, a publishing company based in the Netherlands started selling an eBook (electronic book) on the internet telling about the method we had revealed. Along with much "padding," the book was basically the same as our few paragraphs in our daily tip.

They sold thousands of copies of the eBook for $10.00 each. This company did NOT offer a refund. Their theory was, "Our book reveals the secret. Once you know the secret, you can not give it back... so we are not going to give you your money back under any circumstances."

Well, that company had lots to learn about mail order operations in the United States. No company selling by mail (or online) lasts long here without at least some type of money-back guarantee. The Netherlands company finally bowed to consumer pressure and has started to offer a refund. BUT... at the same time they started to charge $19.95 for their "secret" and have since sold thousands more. Go figure.

Here's the one "secret" that others have paid $10.00 to almost $20.00 for.

We average chewing each bite of our food only about seven times before we swallow it. Start chewing each bite twenty times before you swallow and you will cut your daily calorie intake by about 1000 calories each day.

Yes, it will definitely take some effort and self-discipline to change your lifelong habit of chewing only 7 times... but you can do it. Try it and let us know your results!

If chewing each bite twenty times is simply too much for you... at least double the number of times you chew to about fourteen times and you will still "automatically" cut your daily calorie intake considerably!

4. Here's The Nearest Thing Ever To A "Magic" Weight Loss Potion!

Here's the nearest thing we have to a magic "potion" to help you lose weight. It's a low cost "natural"... it absorbs fat in your stomach... while at the same time telling your brain you are full and don't want any more food! **You can** use it to double the weight you lose with **any** weight loss program.

Many ads you see for weight-loss products lead you to believe they have a "magic-potion"... "Simply take a pill a day and lose 40 pounds this month."

Sorry to say, but there are absolutely no **safe** and sure ways to accomplish such a miracle. Losing weight and keeping it off involves the proper food, exercise and motivation. All these correctly intermingled with common sense can definitely bring you great positive results.

Probably, the nearest thing we have to a "magic potion" is **fiber**. Fiber products act as a sponge in your digestive tract. They fill your tummy and tell your brain you are full. Fiber also **"absorbs" fat** in your stomach and causes it to be excreted instead of being stored in your body!

Most recommendations are that we should get at least 30 to 35 grams of fiber a day simply to keep us healthy. Some authorities go so far as to say we should take in 40 to 60 grams for good weight control.

Ideally, we should get all the fiber we need from food products. Unless you are eating a lot of high fiber cereal, beans and fruit, however, you are probably not getting anywhere near the minimum recommended amount of fiber.

At least one study shows that taking a daily fiber supplement can <u>double the weight loss you get from any weight-loss program</u>.

Natural fiber supplements are available at your local supermarket and/or health food store at a relatively low price. There is no need to pay "an arm and a leg" for some wonder pill you see advertised on television. You must, however, ease into taking such a supplement. Take a teaspoon-a-day this week... and two next week.

Also, if you take any type fiber supplement, it is so very important that you must take it with, and follow it with lots of water.

If you fail to drink enough water with fiber supplements, or even with a high fiber diet, it will have a reverse effect. Your system is likely to become impacted and cause you all sorts of constipation problems.

Here's how fiber in your diet will not only help you lose weight... but may keep you alive!

Fiber is such a very important part of your daily diet. Just what is this thing called dietary fiber.

According the American Heart Association, fiber is, "The term used for several materials that make up the parts of plants your body can't digest. Fiber is classified as soluble or insoluble."

Besides being a great aid in helping us to lose weight, it is also very instrumental in lowering your cholesterol. Any kind of food product that serves two purposes is invaluable to a person trying to lose weight.

Being overweight even in small amounts puts you at risk for heart disease. So, we've got these good foods that help us lose weight, and lower our risk of heart disease. What a great combination!

Fiber is either soluble or insoluble. The front-runner in helping us lower our cholesterol is oats. The foods highest in soluble fiber are oatmeal, oat bran, beans, peas, rice bran, barley, citrus fruits, strawberries and apples.

The insoluble fibers do not seem to help lower cholesterol but they are very important in the aid of normal bowel function... and weight loss. These fibers include whole wheat bread, wheat cereals, wheat bran, rye, rice, barley, and most other grains.

In the fruits and veggies, we find cabbage, beets, carrots, Brussels sprouts, turnips, cauliflower and the skin of the apple (don't peel those apples.)

I have advised you on several occasions to read labels. It is most important when checking on fiber. I have been reading a lot about fiber on cereal boxes and the differences are amazing.

My mother always said, "You need to start your day with a good breakfast."

The best way to get a head start on your fiber is to try one of the following for breakfast:
("c"= calories, "g"= grams) Figures given are for a "serving" which is 1/2 cup.

General Mills Fiber One	65 c,	14 g of fiber
Kellogg's All-Bran Buds	80 c,	13 g of fiber
Kellogg's All-Bran	80 c,	10 g of fiber
Post's 100% Bran	80 c,	8 g of fiber
Kellogg's Raisin Bran	200 c,	8 g of fiber
Post Raisin Bran	190 c,	8 g of fiber.

Fiber from these cereals can give you almost half the fiber you need for the day.

Most of these cereals leave a lot to be desired when it comes to taste. I add fruit and a 90 to 100-calorie fat-free/sugar-free fruit flavored yogurt. The fruit gives you added fiber. Both of these help so much to make your fiber intake more palatable.

Also, yogurt on cereal slows your eating. **Eating slowly causes you to fill up quicker and eat less!** A breakfast of high fiber, fruit and yogurt is very satisfying. It will go a long way toward helping curb the munchies during the rest of your day.

Remember, start out slowly adding fiber to your weight loss program. Most important of all, is to **drink lots and lots of water**!

If you are thinking of using a fiber supplement, please be sure to check with your doctor first. Adding more fiber through food is one thing, but studies show that certain herbal supplements do not mix well with some prescription medicines.

5. Eat One of These "Snacks" Before Every Meal and Reduce Your Calorie Intake by Almost One Third!

Surely you heard the old adage in your childhood that, "An apple a day keeps the doctor away." Like in many old sayings... there is a bushel of truth in this one!

One of the hottest diets touted on the internet right now is the 3-Apple A Day plan advertised by the Gold's Gym institutions. According to them, three apples a day... one before each meal will give you all sort of help in your weight loss program.

We tend to agree with them to some extent.

Apples are a delicious source of dietary fiber to aid digestion and promote weight loss as discussed in secret #4 above. A medium size apple about the size of a tennis ball contains only 80 calories, 5 grams of fiber and almost zero fat or cholesterol. That five grams of fiber is almost twenty percent of the recommended daily fiber intake for the average adult.

Apples contain both soluble and insoluble types of fiber needed to keep your digestive system healthy. The soluble fiber in an apple is Pectin that lubricates the colon and helps ease the elimination of wastes. Pectin also helps prevent cholesterol buildup in your blood vessel walls. The insoluble fiber in apples is primarily in the peel. It helps provide bulk in your digestive system and speed up the movement of food through your digestive system before it is absorbed through the walls of your intestines to be deposited as fat in your body.

Better yet, the complex sweetness of apples helps satisfy your sugar cravings. Apples are also very portable. Keep one in your purse or briefcase for those times when you simply must have a snack between meals.

In addition to its weight loss properties, studies at Mayo Clinic and Cornell University show that a high consumption of apples may reduce colon cancer by 43 percent and lung cancer by as much as 50 percent! That alone induces me to make sure I get lots of apples in my daily diet! Mayo Clinic also found a correlation between apple consumption and the prevention of prostate cancer in men.

It just gets better and better! Several European studies show that a diet rich in apples also helps prevent strokes and heart disease.

You should not, of course, consume the core and seeds of your apples... but you will do well to always eat your apples peel and all. What type apple is best for your weight loss efforts? It doesn't matter. Go to your grocery and buy one of several available to choose the one you like best. Or... swap up types to eliminate boredom.

Speaking of boredom... we suggest that you do not stick to the 3 apples a day bit more than a couple of days before you break up the monotony by having a bowl of Souper Soup before several meals instead of apples.

Don't forget... if you are on a balanced diet as we recommend with your divided plate... you can also substitute Souper Soup for one complete meal on some days.

Beware... this substitution is not part of the Souper Soup quick weight loss plan. Use it in addition to your regular healthy (at least two) balanced meals each day--- after you're off the seven day Souper Soup regimen.

6. An Almost FREE Item That Helps You Take Off Pounds and Inches Effortless!

Healthy people stay healthy by drinking water. It's low cost... (nearly free) and is so very good for you. No weight loss plan is complete without the consumption of at least 6 to 8 eight-ounce glasses of water each day. This is mandatory if you are on a high fiber diet.

You will do well to drink a glass of water about ten minutes before each meal. Like the apple or bowl of soup discussed earlier... this is one of those little things that will squelch your appetite, satisfy your desire for food while cutting your food consumption and calories considerably.

Did you know that drinking ice water instead of tap temperature water actually makes you lose weight. The reason for this miraculous fact is that fat calories are burned to bring the water temperature up to an internal 98.6 degrees F. temperature.

When you drink water that's 40 degrees or colder, your body has to raise the water's temperature to your body temperature. It burns about 1 calorie per ounce of water in doing so. One report shows even better results from eating ice. (Just be sure not to break your teeth!)

With only an average intake of **cold** water, you should lose about 6 ½ pounds in a year at no cost or effort.

One of our readers, Betty shared a great tip on drinking water.

She said, "I have trouble drinking a full glass of water. By keeping a 4 oz. paper cup in the bathroom, I find it is easy to drink one, and usually another of the small cups. I don't know why the smaller size is easier to drink than a full 8 oz. or more glass, but it is!

7. Activity (Exercise)

Many of us do not even like the sound of the word "exercise." Sometime back... in Lillie's Tips we started using the term "activity" instead of exercise.

Seriously, you need some type of activity at least three or more times a week. For an aerobic type activity I recommend a brisk 30 minute walk. Add to this stretching exercises before you start and after to help prevent injury.

Also, strength training is important. You don't have to be a weight lifter. It can be as simple as carrying jugs of water from the basement. This is what keeps my very active older sister so very fit. She also goes for a walk before breakfast... rain or shine... sleet or northern New York state snow.

Make Your Activity/Exercise a Fun Time: Boredom is the death of any weight loss/exercise program. Diversify your activities with dancing, swimming, bicycling, or gardening. Make it something you already like to do.

If you walk, vary your walking routes. If you walk out of doors, change to mall walking for a few days. It will keep you from getting bored with your program.

Carry a tape or CD player with your favorite music. Or, you may purchase music especially designed just for walking.

You do not have to exercise for 30 minutes at a time. Instead, doing so for five or ten minutes can be done on a break or at lunch--- or walking through the mall while you're shopping.

Put those walking shoes where you can get to them easily. Breaking your exercise into these short intervals will help you lose weight just as fast. Maybe even faster, because you will probably stick to the program longer.

Consider joining an exercise program. There are a lot of programs in which you can participate. Some have a cost, but many churches and organizations offer free programs. Suggest this to your boss.

Exercise with a buddy. Get a friend to meet you in the park. Good chance to enjoy their company, plus, the time will go so much faster.

When you add exercise to your day, you can greet your family with a much better disposition. And, you will rest so much better at night.

Park your car at the edge of the mall parking lot. Take a lap around inside the mall when you are doing your shopping. Do you have leaves or maybe snow in your area? Getting rid of those two will certainly help with your program.

When talking on the telephone, take that wireless phone or cell phone and ride an exercise bike that is sitting in the corner gathering dust. Get up off that couch and turn the TV station instead of using that remote.

At work... take those stairs instead of the elevator. Park in the farthest parking space at work, the mall, or anywhere you go. If you are a golfer, walk that course instead of using the cart. Instead of going to a car wash (and if the weather permits).... wash that car manually.

You will be very surprised at just how many hundreds of calories such small activities will burn over the course of a year... and how many pounds and inches you could remove!

Chapter Five

Motivativational Secrets and Mind Tricks

8. The number one priority you should never lose sight of when trying to lose weight.

Make **you**, your number one priority. So the bed doesn't get made first thing or there's a little dust. (Turn the lights down when you have company and the dust will create a little ambiance) :-)

Plan your menus, find the time to exercise and you will feel so good about yourself. And everything else will take its proper place.

Always make **you** the primary reason for losing weight. You can use other people... other things (such as a special occasion... wedding... class reunion, etc.) for losing weight, but the only way you are going to keep it off is to do if for yourself.

Only **you** can keep any weight-loss program going.

9. Why your scale may not give you the best indication of your weight loss success.

Measurements of Success:

The scales sometimes become such a nemesis for us. We make it the "be all and end all" of our weight loss success.

Don't make the proverbial scale the only measurement of your weight-loss success. Consider those skirts or pants that you couldn't button a few weeks ago.

How about that well appreciated complement from a friend, ("You've lost weight!")

Savor that great feeling you get when you cross your legs and they don't rub together any more. Appreciate the fact that you're no longer breathless when you walk.

The scale isn't always a total indication of how well you are doing. When you exercise regularly, you build muscles and they **do** weigh more than fat. But, they help you look sooooo much better!

One big "no-no" is... weighing yourself every single day. When my scales are handy, I too find myself checking my weight once or sometimes more times each day. Don't! It can be very discouraging, to say the least.

There are so many factors that change our weight on a daily basis.

Factors such as, how much liquid you have had or the fact that you have started a new exercise program.

And for us ladies, at certain times of the month, our bodies retain more liquid causing us to weigh more.

There are many factors such as time of day, or how much liquid you have consumed and not eliminated that can effect your weight on a day-to-day basis.

This can be very depressing, if you find that one day you are down and the next day you are up..., when you are being so careful with your weight loss plan.

Make it a point to weigh the same time of day and the same day each week... **once each week**. Make it a Special Occasion.

Like a lot of other things... put that scale out-of-sight-and-out-of-mind.

10. How to deal with "saboteurs," those pencil thin people who are always urging you to eat fattening foods.

Sabotage! Watch out for those "feeder" people who think you are getting too thin. At your next family or friend "get-together," they will always have your favorite foods on hand and will prod you into eating something you would really like to avoid.

These saboteurs are usually very thin or jealous folks. Usually, they are the latter. Bring your own dessert or casserole so you will have something you can (should) eat. As the people who warn you against using drugs say it... "Just say no!"

You may also reply with a big smile and, "No thank you, I am allergic to it... it makes me fat." This is my daughters favorite comeback to the "saboteurs."

11. Here's the very best way you can relieve stress.

Stress can be both a positive time and a negative time in our lives. A wedding or a new baby is a joyful time, but they are stressful nonetheless. These times can be pitfalls in our weight loss efforts.

We are busy and **think** we don't have the time for ourselves, but making time to eat properly and exercise can be the most successful thing you can do to relieve stress.

Remember, you are **number one** and that is **not** being selfish. You will find that by doing these things for yourself, you will have more time for family and friends!

12. The clothes you should never keep in your closet.

Don't keep "fat clothes" in your closet. Give them to a shelter, church or any charitable organization. Or have a garage/tag sale. Don't think that you might need them again... because if you do think that way... you probably **will** need them again.

Get rid of those clothes that are too big now. What are you saving them for? Just in case you might need them again? Turn that kind of thinking in to a more positive attitude. Tell yourself that you are not going to need them and send them to your favorite charity.

When shopping for clothes, don't buy them big. Make sure that they fit. Nothing makes you look bigger than those over-sized clothes. I know they are comfortable, but look the best you can while losing weight. It will make you feel so much better about yourself.

Try shopping resale shops for clothes while losing weight. These are temporary clothes... right? You can resell them as you lose.

13. Why you should always share your weight loss success stories with another person.

Share Your Successes: It is great for your own motivation, but it also can be of help to someone .

Share some of your weight loss strategies with another person who is trying to lose weight. They too may have some great information that will help you in your program. To share information on a "grand scale," make sure you are connected to the internet and pay a visit to:

Lillie's Weight Loss Support Group at:
http://www.lillieross.com/support.htm

You'll love it!

14. How to use the power of imagination to become that thin sexy person you want to be.

Visualize: **See** yourself finishing the race. Do this even in your daily exercise.

The same is true in your weight loss efforts. Visualize yourself as that thin sexy person you want to be... and you soon will be! Shut your eyes and picture in your mind the body you want to create.

When I was a kid, I was long, lean and clumsy. My siblings and peers called me "Grace." I grew up thinking I was about the most awkward thing that came down the pike.

This self image of myself carried over to my later days when I was no longer lean. I felt that I was about the worst looking thing around. My self-image and self-talk were very negative to say the least.

I still find myself on occasion, putting myself down. This is a sure fire way to defeat any positive thoughts I might have about weight loss efforts or maintaining my weight.

We all need to take a more affirmative approach to our weight loss efforts. Positive statements should be a part of our daily life. When negative thoughts pop into your mind, say, "I can do anything I set my mind to including losing weight!"

I've always been somewhat of a believer in "mind-over-matter"... but **I know it works** when the "matter" involved is one's own body.

Remember the "Little Engine" who thought he could? Just think you can and.... YOU CAN.

Believe you can and you WILL do it!

15. How using "positive feedback" can help take off pounds and inches from your body.

Rewards: With each accomplishment you make, such as your first five pounds or each five pounds--- reward yourself with a non-food treat.

This "positive feedback" doesn't have to cost anything. Read that book you have wanted to read for a long time. Take a loooooong bubble bath. Go for a meditative walk. Visit an elderly friend. (You both will be rewarded.)

16. Psychological tricks to help you keep the weight off after you've lost it.

One of the hardest things to do in getting thin, is to stay that way. I feel sometimes that we get too caught up with the idea of losing the weight.

Then, when we get to our goal, we lose sight of our purpose of losing in the first place, and think we are finished. We still need to watch what we eat, stay motivated and active.

So keep in touch with my daily tips. Keep going to those groups that helped you lose weight, read those labels, keep in touch with the people that were supportive of your weight loss efforts and ask us to help you stay at your goal and healthy.

17. Here's a "do unto others" trick to help you through those times when you slip up, eat entirely too much and become depressed.

All or Nothing Attitude: We all have days when we want that special dessert or entree, and know that we have already eaten more than we feel we should have.

We then have a tendency to beat ourselves up and become depressed. The first thing we do is head for the refrigerator and eat more-- and we become more depressed. We then say, "I can't do it!" And we give up!

Think what you would say to someone else that was having this problem. You would not allow them to beat themselves up, would you? You would be understanding and supportive. You would help them through this.

So... be as kind to yourself as you are to others. Just know you are human and we all slip sometimes.

18. Easy to do secrets of beating a binge eating habit.

Feelings and binge eating: Keep a log or write in your journal about the times you binge and determine what it was that set you off. Was it hurt feelings, anger or possibly loneliness?

If you can go to the source of your problem, perhaps it will help you get through the next temptation to binge. If it is anger or hurt feelings, perhaps you should confront the person.

If this isn't possible, or you don't want to do it--- just write what you might say to the person. Putting these emotions down on paper, even if you don't send them, can help clear the air for you.

I know of someone close to me who recently broke off a relationship. She sat down and wrote all things that were wrong with the involvement. Even though this person didn't send this letter to anyone, she told me that it was such a great release.

This person has turned to food most of her life when emotions ran high and this was a great way for her to let the feelings go without binging.

If loneliness is your problem, try getting involved with other people that might need you, such as residents of a nursing home. Talk about lonely! Some of these people have families who never come to see them. This will take your mind off yourself and it is so rewarding.

I found myself lonely several years ago. A wise person told me to find someone who needed me more than I needed myself. I did and it worked!

We all tend to overeat or "pig out" from time to time. This is not necessarily binge eating disorder, which is a very serious medical problem. The first and most important thing, is that if you think that you have this disorder, get help from a health professional immediately. Talk with your doctor and get him/her to refer you to someone trained in treating binge eating.

This is not a problem you **alone** have, or that you can solve **alone**. And guess what... you girls out there... we do it more often than the guys. But the good news in all this, is that most people do well in treatment and can overcome binge eating. So know there is help out there for you.

Please, please check with your doctor. This is most important!

19. Here's how you can be stronger than the urge to eat a whole box of cookies or carton of ice cream.

The Influence of Food: Are you not bigger than that whole box of cookies or whole carton of ice cream?

Do you find that little package of candy or chips has the muscle to make a big person like you not put it down! Does it have the ability to call you from the pantry or refrigerator and send you headed in that direction?

Take control of the situation **now**. **You make the choice to eat**! Don't let the food do it for you.

Find something else to do. Go for a walk, call a friend, take a shower or post a message on **Lillie's Weight Loss Support Group** at http://www.lillieross.com/support.htm

20. Here's how you can "talk to yourself" to help you lose weight.

Talking to one's self: Sound like a little bit nuts? Not so. When you find yourself in front of the "fridge" contemplating eating something, ask yourself-- Am I really hungry or just mindlessly eating?

We often mistake hunger for thirst. This is good time to drink a big glass of water or have a cup of herbal tea... wait ten minutes and then decide if you really are hungry.

21. Six "reminder" triggers to help you lose weight.

REMINDERS:

1. You don't have to clean your plate.

2. You do have to slow down eating. Remember it takes twenty minutes for your brain to know you are full.

3. Eat the **five-a-day** (veggies and fruits)

4. Participate in your favorite activities (exercise)

5. And, be kind to yourself! Do not beat yourself up If you don't get it just right.

6. Hey--- don't forget--- we're all human.

22. Here is a perfect example of why you should never DIET to lose weight.

Have you ever noticed that the first three letters of DIET spell DIE? Don't you feel that you are going to do just that some time when you are trying to DIET?

Change your approach or mind set to a more positive approach. Think of losing weight as a new life style. Think of it as slimming down, **not** as a DIET. **Call it something else!**

Put a positive twist to your weight loss program. And the process will be so much easier.

23. Learn why depriving yourself of something you really love can be death to a weight loss program.

Deprivation is a two-edged sword. It can be death to a weight loss program. It can lead to binge eating.

Do you remember as a child the things to which Mother said no? Seemed to be just what you wanted the most, didn't it?

The same is true as adults.

Have a little of the special flavor creamers in your coffee.

Order a dessert when you go out for a special meal, and share it with the others at the table.

Order the house salad dressing on the side and remember to dip your fork into the dressing and then into your salad. You get a lot less high calorie dressing, but that good flavor is there.

Be good to yourself!

24. Tempted to cheat on your weight loss plan? Here's a "mind game" to help you resist the temptation.

I belong to a bowling league. Each member of our team puts a quarter into a bank every time they miss a spare. At the end of the year, we have enough money to pay our fees to the state tournament from these savings.

I thought I could apply this to my weight loss efforts by using the same principle when I feel inclined to "cheat."

Get a bank and every time you feel like you want to cheat with high calorie food, put in a nickel, dime, quarter or whatever amount that you think might keep you from eating that food.

But, before you drop that money into the bank, decide if you really want to "cheat" and if this "cheating" is worth the cost--- both financial, and to your diet.

If you don't "cheat," put that money back in your pocket and **pat yourself on the back.**

25. How you can enjoy Thanksgiving or Christmas dinner without absolutely blowing your weight loss plan.

The "big" eating day here in the USA is Thanksgiving.

We all have so much to be thankful for. Most of us have plenty to eat. And, we all seem to over do it.

Don't deprive yourself on this holiday. Eat some of the things you really like in smaller portions. Get out a salad plate instead of a dinner plate. Get only **one** plateful. Don't go back for seconds.

Go for a walk or get in some kind of extra activity that will help you burn those calories. Don't settle in front of the TV for the whole afternoon and night.

But most important of all... **don't beat yourself up** if you overdo it. Just pick yourself up on Friday, dust yourself off, and start back on your program.

26. How an actress in a famous movie can help you "pick yourself up" and start over when you fail in your weight loss efforts.

Was a holiday weekend such as Thanksgiving overwhelming? Is that food still hanging around. How about sharing leftovers, if there are any.

Also, remember not to beat yourself up if you overindulged.

Don't look back! Always look forward. So you ate an extra piece of cake. It doesn't have to be or shouldn't be an excuse to stop. It's done. It's a very small set back. Take the "Scarlett" attitude from "Gone With the Wind"---- Tomorrow is most definitely another day. So, pick yourself right back up and start all over again.

Another holiday season looms close behind and the days will pass quickly. I have found that some time I even do better this time of the year with my weight loss efforts, because I am so busy with all the hustle bustle of the season that I don't get around to eating so much and often. But be careful not to go tooooo long without eating and over eat when you finally get around to it.

Be good to yourself. Don't let all of this send you into an eating frenzy.

Let your health and well being be the **number one** priority--- and all the rest will fall into place.

27. How you can conquer snack-attack and midnight-refrigerator-raid temptations.

Raiding the refrigerator at midnight? Overwhelmed by snack attacks?

We all have special cravings from time to time. Sometimes we want something sweet. Sometimes it is something salty we crave.

Planning ahead for these times is so very important. Have the light or air popcorn on hand to microwave. Make up the sugar free, fat free gelatin puddings and put them in individual bowls. Top them off with fat free whipped toppings. Make them look attractive.

Being prepared for snacks or any hunger is so important. Otherwise, we have the tendency to eat more and it is usually something we really didn't want to eat in the first place, but we were soooo hungry!

It is so important to be prepared.

28. Why you should make New Year "choices" instead of "resolutions."

As we approach the beginning of a new year, we all begin to make those resolutions!

The number one resolution people make is to lose weight. And, it is probably the easiest resolution to break.

Instead of making the choice of losing weight a resolution--- Make it just that--- a choice. Don't make it something that you are going to feel guilty about, if you can't follow it to the letter.

We get so caught up in trying to be perfect in our weight loss efforts, that at the least setback, we give up.

Set realistic goals for your weight loss. Don't make them so overwhelming that they can't be achieved. Don't look back! Always look forward.

So you ate an extra piece of cake. It doesn't have to be or shouldn't be an excuse to stop. It's done. It's a very small set back. Take the "Scarlett" attitude ---- Tomorrow is most definitely another day. So, pick yourself right back up and start all over again.

29. How to avoid addictive and unsatisfying "goodies" you know are bad for your weight loss efforts.

Do you find yourself feeling like my daughter and me after a holiday. We were talking about the food we had eaten during the holidays, and how it was both addictive and unsatisfying.

We both felt after we had eaten something sweet and rich that we wanted more and more--- and that we became bottomless pits. It just didn't satisfy.

We both regrouped from all the heavy holiday eating and ate a wonderful grilled chicken salad. We commented how much easier it is to fill up on good, healthy fruits, vegetables, and lean meats.

A week after the holidays and back onto healthy food, I felt much better and had more energy.

It makes you wonder why we think we have to change our eating habits for the holidays, doesn't it?

30. Here's a trick to help you buy groceries for a spouse, roommate, child, etc. who is pencil thin without tempting yourself to partake of their treats.

Shopping can cause great anxiety for us folks who are trying to lose weight.

This is especially true when you have someone in your family who is pencil thin and accompanies you to the market. They can make the trip a virtual nightmare for you.

So you have a spouse, roommate, child, etc. who is skinny and does not have a weight problem. You buy the groceries and they want all the high fat, high calorie food.

When you get home from shopping, package these "weight gainers" in individual packages. Or, buy them in the individual packages. Then get them out of your sight!

Also, try to buy the candies, cookies and treats that you really don't like and can live without.

Here are some of the things that work for me when grocery shopping.

First make a list and stick to it. Use the list like a map of the store. If the first thing you come to is fruits and veggies, put that first on the list--- and so on around the store.

Avoid certain aisles. You know the ones--- candies, cookies, chips, etc.

Never get in a hurry when shopping.

The end of a busy, tiring, stressful work day can be another time that may lead you to impulse buying.

Never, ever, shop when you are starving hungry! And, if possible, always shop alone.

31. An easy way to make eating a real pleasure while eating less. OR An easy meal time habit that helps satisfy your hunger without overeating.

Satisfaction: Do you find yourself wondering what you are going to eat the next meal before you complete the one you are eating?

Sound familiar? It is important to take the time with each meal to make sure that you are getting enough to eat and you are satisfied. Skipping meals and not eating enough will only lend to binge eating.

Slow Down! This is a rush-rush life and we find ourselves swallowing our food whole to get back to work. Take time to enjoy your meals as much as possible. Your tummy tum-tum takes twenty minutes before it knows you have had enough to eat. Woofing your food only leads to overeating.

Conscious eating is such an important part of our weight loss efforts. We should be aware of every bite we put in our mouth.

We all live in a rush, rush world. We wolf down our food. We don't make eating a pleasure.

Have you ever (and I have been guilty of this) eaten a whole bag of cookies or chips without even realizing that you have done it... until you are shaking the bag for those last few crumbs?

When you are eating a meal, try to make it the only thing you are doing. Don't sit in front of the TV. I have seen people in restaurants reading while eating. Wait until another time to call someone for a chat, not at mealtime. And, don't work while eating.

Savor each and every bite at a table away from the TV and work. Put that fork down between bites. Remember, someone--- maybe you, went to the trouble of preparing the meal--- so enjoy.

I know you are saying, if I don't eat at my desk I might not get to eat. But, try as often as possible to find another location to eat.

Remember, eating should not be just our source of fuel... it should be a pleasure. With this slowing and enjoying each bite you will find yourself eating much less.

32. Did you know that going hungry will cause you to gain weight. Here's why.

Did you know that if you don't eat enough food, your metabolism will slow down to the point that you will **not** lose weight... Your brain will tell your body, "Hey you, no way am I going to allow you starve me to death!"

SO, don't go hungry! It doesn't pay in any shape, form or fashion.

My readers are such an inspiration... I really appreciate all the great tips they share.

Betty tells us, "One of the things that has kept me going when I have had a "bad" week is to measure my body and compare those amounts with where I was when I started -- or even where I was 2-3 months ago. What a difference! Inches make the difference!

Another thing that helped me was when I finally broke down and bought some clothes that fit. Granted, these were "previously owned, but lovely."

Thank you Betty!

We all need to remember our accomplishments when we seem to hit those inevitable plateaus.

33. How to avoid the weight gaining urges instilled in us by the genes we inherited from our cave-man ancestors.

I was brought up by a mother who lived through the Great Depression of the '30s. We were taught to be very frugal, and especially with food. Also, when I first got married we really had to scrimp on groceries... and I got very creative with making food stretch.

In more prosperous times I found myself wanting to eat every high priced, high calorie food in sight. The result was over eating and gaining weight.

This may be something that is inborn... something that goes back to our ancestral "cave man" days and the survival of the fittest. We need to fight those "inner pulls" and come up with alternative things to do when they rear their ugly head.

If it's a social event and you know the tables will be loaded with irresistible delicacies you didn't have in your younger days, try eating something before going. A bowl of Souper Soup and an apple would be ideal. Don't go hungry. When you get there... get something to drink and stay away from that table!

Possibly your friends, neighbors, or co-workers bring you "goodies" you just can't resist. If you don't want to hurt feelings, try a little and tell them you will save the rest for later... and then get rid of it.

When we get those "cave man urges" (eat all you can today because you may not eat again for days)... let's recognize them for what they are and be more selective in what we eat!

34. Here's a mother's advice that helps you lose weight, feel better and sleep better.

My readers keep me awake at night trying to come up with new tips for them? :-)

Recently, about 2 o'clock in the morning, I remembered some advice my mother gave me a long time ago. As mother's go, she was very wise. And, you have to know, this was long before we became aware of low-fat, low-calorie, no-sugar, healthy eating.

Mother's advice was to, "Eat breakfast like a king, lunch like a rich man and supper like a pauper." Growing up, that is exactly how we ate. She prepared a large breakfast. Our lunch was all the good veggies, meat, and bread sources that we needed.

But for supper, she was true to her saying. We had supper like PAUPERS. Supper was usually very light. And guess what? I was very, very thin!

I have been trying to follow my Mother's advice lately and find that I feel so much better. I don't get as hungry before lunch, and I sleep better not having such a heavy supper. Maybe you won't keep me awake now? :-)

35. How the simple child's game of "Mother May I" can help you lose weight.

Here I go again relating to my childhood. They say once a man (or woman) and twice a child. Do you suppose that's what happening to me?

There was a game we used to play called "Mother May I." As I remember, the leader said take so many "giant" steps and you had to say, "May I?" to move forward. The other command was to take so many "baby" steps, and again you had to say, "May I?" or you didn't move forward.

In our weight loss efforts, we try to take **giant** steps to reach our goal. We want to be slim and trim by "yesterday."

Instead, we need to start by taking those **baby** steps. We need that one-day-at-a-time attitude. Let's set goals that are attainable and applaud our daily successes.

In something I recently read or saw on television, the question was asked, "How do you eat an elephant?"

The answer? "One bite at a time."

Ask yourself, "May I?"

Then move forward toward your goal with each step.

36. When you need inspiration in continuing your weight loss efforts... remember these children's stories.

Children's stories are a great inspiration for some of the things we need to remember in our weight loss efforts.

One such story that comes to mind is "The Tortoise and the Hare." We should make our changes to our weight lose efforts slowly and steadily.

That Hare thought he could rush through the race to the finish line and beat that old slow poke turtle. But, the pokey turtle just hung in there and persisted... until he beat the hare and won the race.

Be like that Tortoise and go the distance... even on the days when you think you've lost race.

Our reader, Bev wrote, "One thing you left out of this story is: the hare thinking he had a lot of time - laid down and took a nap. The moral of this story is you can't lay down on the job. Which is a good moral to losing weight!!"

So true.

37. When it is OK to say NO to Mom!

It is not always what we are eating that causes our weight loss problems. It is what is eating us!

We have the food pushers, like Mom... clean your plate... poor people starving... I made this just for you. Can't disappoint Mom. Right?

WRONG! Say NO to MOM. I know it is hard. Say it in a nice way. Thank her for going to the trouble and that you appreciate her efforts, but please save it for someone else until you are able to eat the food in a controlled situation.

There are even positive stressful situations like a new baby in the house that keeps us at the frig eating. When we are overly tired we mistake hunger for rest that we need. Hand off some of the responsibility of a new baby. Grandma's like to take charge. Or even Dad. Get some needed rest.

You will feel so much better when you return. It will keep you away from the dreaded fridge.

It is so true that FOOD is a pacifier... a comforter. The only person in any of these situations that is hurt is YOU!

You need to be the most important person in these situations. You are the only one that can control them.

Letting the situation control YOU is the downfall of any weight loss program.

38. Where to place a mirror to help you lose weight

Sometimes we just need something to stop us before we go off the deep end with our eating... something that stops us in our tracks before we get started!

Prevention magazine tells us to put a mirror in your dining room as a deterrent to over eating. Can't you just imagine yourself setting down to eat and seeing your reflection putting that food in your mouth?

I have a mirror near my kitchen table. I am going to sit where I can see me eating. I'll let you know how it works for me.

39. Times when it is OK to indulge in your favorite food... no matter how decadent!

Occasionally we need to give ourselves permission to indulge. We get so bored sometimes with our weight loss plans... and this can be a time when we just might hang it up.

The weekend may be a good time to plan for such a "permission." Weekends are when we might have a family get-together. There are always those temptation foods. If you plan ahead to have that special indulgence and make it something you are looking forward to, you will be less likely to eat more than you bargained for.

Remember, when we don't eat something that we really like from time to time, we sometimes end up eating more calories from something else that really didn't satisfy that craving.

Be good to yourself. Have a little something special. Then jump right back into your program and eat less the next day... and/or add more activity.

40. Here's how to keep special occasions such as birthdays, weddings, etc. from blowing your weight loss plan

Special occasions are one of the hardest things to deal with on any weight loss program.

You have gotten into the swing of the weight loss program that you are on. You have gotten your motivation level up. Then, BANG along comes a birthday, a wedding, an anniversary, holidays... whatever.

You over-indulge. You feel guilty. They just seem to set you back, sometimes even to the point of giving up on your weight loss efforts.

Before attending or having a special event, make the first priority YOU. Plan for the extra eating. Eat less for a few days before the event as well as on the day of event.

Eat before you go. Having your meal before you attend will cut your appetite and those tempting goodies will not be so tempting if you are already full.

If you are having the event, make sure there are some of your favorite low calorie foods available.

Most of all, if you do overeat, don't beat yourself up. Putting yourself on a guilt trip can just lead to more overeating. Simply restart your program the next day or even the same day, if the event is in the morning. Don't miss a beat with your plan. As they say, "just get right back on that horse."

41. Could science have this real "magic pill" on its way to taking off our excess weight?

We sometimes long for the day when we can take a "magic pill" and those extra pounds just melt away. The big news lately concerning weight loss is that scientists have isolated a hormone called PPY3-36 that makes you feel full when you eat.

Studies show that the people tested ate a third less and went as long as 12 hours without snacking.

This "magic pill" is not ready for general use. There are many tests to see what long term effects this might have on the body. If our dear Federal Drug Administration acts as usual... we're probably talking about five or six years before it is available in the U.S.

There are all kinds of things that have been offered to lose weight... from pills to stomach stapling. None are effective on the long haul unless we make changes to our eating and activity life styles.

The real "magic pill" is to make a life time commitment to healthy eating and activity.

Reprogramming your eating habits is so important. Learning to choose healthy, nutritious, low-fat foods and adding activity on a regular basis is the only real way to go with your weight loss efforts.

You did not become overweight in a day and it is not going to come off or stay off without commitment. It is difficult to look very far into the future. The first step is to make it a day by day commitment and one day you won't even have to think about eating healthy. It "suddenly" becomes a part of you.

42. Didn't lose any weight last week? Here's how to handle that!

You think you have had a great week. You have been so very careful with everything you have eaten.

You got those veggies and fruits into your program. You have had your six to eight glasses of water. You have put some kind of daily activity in your program.

You are in the process of patting yourself on the back... and you get to the scales and you haven't lost! Wow!! What a downer!

There are some weeks when you may not lose no matter how careful you have been. It can be the demise of a weight loss program, if you let it. To me this is one thing that can make you want to give up. DON"T!!

Remember, don't consider the scales as your Number ONE mark of success on your weight loss program?

Do what I said at the first about those wonderful things you did for yourself? You ate lots of healthy foods. You drank your water. You put activity in your life. You have NOT FAILED, if you have done some or all of these things. Changing even one old habit is SUCCESS!

Booker T. Washington once said, "Success is to be measured not so much by the position that one has reached in life as by the obstacles which he has overcome."

Consider the fact that not losing weight is just an obstacle on the way to success in your weight loss program. Don't give up!!

43. Could the right kind of china help you lose weight?

My mother as well as my mother-in-law both used to "save" their "good" dishes. For what? I will never know.

I have found over the years that setting a pretty table can really make a "weight loss meal" so very much more appealing.

Paper plates are certainly handy... and I have been known to stand up and eat a meal.

But at least once a day, try setting a table, as if company were coming. Go in your yard and bring in a few flowers, or move some artificial ones from another part of the house. Get out a pretty placemat or tablecloth.

Come to think of it, nothing is any prettier than fresh salad veggies arranged on a nice plate. Or, fruit in maybe a bowl or glass with a stem. (Both are on any weight loss plan.)

Isn't it great fun when you are at someone else's home and they have brought their good things out for you?

It will take only a few minutes more to make your meal special. You are worth it! Get your family involved with setting the table. I'll bet your family will be surprised and appreciate it also.

So what are you saving those "good" dishes for?

44. Why "Southern" ladies say it is not polite to lick the platter clean.

Even after all these years, one thing my mother used to say to me that still rings in my ears is "Clean your plate." You know... "all those starving children in China." I still simply hate to waste food.

It's some time difficult not to clean my plate even when I'm full. This also goes for things like microwave popcorn, packages of cookies, carton's of ice cream. Clean it all up. Don't waste food. It is like there is no tomorrow. Gotta get all in today. Can't save any for tomorrow.

Over the years one thing I have observed about thin family members and friends is that they DO resist the urge to clean their plates, eat the whole bag of cookies or carton of ice cream. They leave food on their plates. They take only one or two cookies etc.

It is difficult to unlearn things what we were taught as children, but it can be done. For foods that I can't control my eating... I don't keep in the house but get occasionally when dining out.

Using smaller plates and not going back for seconds is a big help. Share desserts with someone else. If you have family members who can eat anything, package foods in smaller containers and get them out of sight as soon as they come in the house. "Out of sight...Out of mind."

Another thing that helps... do you remember how Mom always said to eat your veggies first? Look at your plate and choose the low calorie foods such as your veggies to eat first. Then eat the next highest and so on.

Save your highest calorie foods to eat last. By the time you get to them... you just might be too full to finish them all!

My older sister said someone told her a long time ago that a "Southern lady" always leaves a little something on her plate. She said is not polite to "lick the platter clean." :-) So I try to remember what this wise lady said when tempted to clean my plate and I know that I am full.

Our reader Pam had this sage bit of advice on about leaving food on your plate.

"I have found that it helps me to remember that the food left over after I am full is going one of two places:

1) if I DON'T eat it, it will go to WASTE
2) if I DO eat it, it will go to WAIST!

So, it is going to waste/waist either way! I am trying to choose #1 a lot more often."

45. Use this secret to pick yourself up when you are really down on yourself about your lack of weight loss.

So many times, we get so very tired of trying to lose weight. It is a constant battle and we just wish we could eat just any old thing and still lose weight.

Worse yet, we often do just that! We eat any old thing and we find ourselves kicking ourselves, major guilt trips, and ultimately quitting our efforts.

I ran across a few very helpful quotations on this subject of quitting... and thought they might be helpful to you if or when you are thinking of giving up. The first is from Kathleen Norris, poet and author.

"Before you begin a thing, remind yourself that difficulties and delays quite impossible to foresee are ahead. If you could see them clearly, naturally you could do a great deal to get rid of them, but you can't.

You can only see one thing clearly and that is your goal. Form a mental vision of that and cling to it through thick and thin."

Staying centered on your goal to lose weight is so very important.

Norman Vincent Peale said, "It's always too early to quit."

This is so true. Many times I have seen people very close to their goal give up just when success is right around the corner.

And finally from Napoleon Hill, "Effort only fully releases its reward after a person refuses to quit."

We can reap the reward of success in our weight loss journey, if we just keep trying.

46. Upset because you only lost a pound or two this week? Use this secret to get yourself in the right frame of mind!

The thing I used to hear the most as a weight loss leader, and now from my readers is... "I'm doing terrible... I only lost a half pound or one pound or five pounds this week."

If you have been with me for awhile, you've read this before. BUT... we need to remind ourselves when we are feeling discouraged about our losses just how a half pound or one pound or five pounds really looks... and also how much five pounds extra on our body feels like.

I am one for visuals. If I can see it, I usually can believe it.

Go to the frig or a store and look at a pound of margarine/butter or a pound of hamburger. When you lose "only 1 pound," that's four less sticks or patties you have on your "bod". :-)

Carry five pounds of flour or sugar around your home for even 10 or 15 minutes. You'll feel MUCH better when you put it down... just like you feel better each time you lose a pound or five pounds or even a half pound.

Any time the scales show you are losing **anything**... that is one more step toward your goal. **Celebrate** instead of being discouraged!!

47. Do you have a food that sends you straight to the refrigerator? Here's how to handle it.

Do you know what triggers an eating frenzy for you?

Making a list of foods that trigger your eating frenzies and posting it in a convenient place like cabinets or refrigerators is a great way to get a handle on this problem. If you know what is causing the problem, you can avoid it all together or find an alternative to eating it.

Maybe go for a walk. Visit a friend. Or get really busy with something you love doing... your hobby... reading a book... visiting with love ones... whatever pleases you.

48. A 10-minute mental trick keeps you from over eating.

Give It 10 Minutes Before You Indulge!"

Laurie added how waiting ten minutes before giving in to an eating urge helped her. I would like to share her letter with you

"This is a great little trick that I had long forgotten! I used this to quit smoking years ago... My boss told me (promised me) I could have that cigarette in 45 minutes and he would not challenge me at all.

You know what happened? About an hour and a half went by before I remembered the "deal"... I was so amazed that I decided to put off that cigarette for another 45 minutes... days and days and years went by.

I also used to do this with food when I was just having the munchies... I would promise myself that I would go get my snack in 20 minutes.

Then I would sit down with a book and next thing I knew an hour would go by and I didn't even miss the cookies or chips or whatever...

Or, you might create some kind of ceremony. For instance you will say, "I am not going to let this cookie (trigger food) get the best of me." Look at your watch and wait ten minutes. This is very helpful if you are really not hungry, but think you've just got to have that chocolate chip cookie. Chances are that you will decide it really isn't worth the extra calories.

Thanks for reminding me about this great little mental trick! I am going to re-activate the program!"

Some of the simplest tips work... Why not give this a try in your weight loss effort?

Here's a perfect example of "If you can see it... you can believe it!"

As we are preparing to go to press with this book... Daily Weight Loss Tips subscriber, Robert wrote us in response to our tip about using visuals to help with our weight loss journey. Robert says:

"At 56, I'm 6'3" and weigh 225 although last summer I had it down to 199 from a high of 310 in my late 40's. "Ahhh, " I thought, "what's 25 pounds more or less?"

The other day, I was working in my backyard with a 20# sledge hammer driving some metal stakes down so my lawn mower wouldn't eat them and bend the blades. "Whew," I thought, "this sure is heavy. I wouldn't want to carry this around all day."

Then it hit me: I AM carrying it around. Now I leave that sledge by the refrigerator to remind myself what's at stake.

By the way -- your "Souper Soup" and a diet of vegetables, fruit, and fish got me from 310 to 199."

Your testimonial, Robert, is probably the best we have received in the past three years. Thanks! If we have in any way helped anyone else lose more than 111 pounds... please let me know! This sort of thing makes my day... and my job so worthwhile!

Chapter Six

Food and Recipe Secrets

49. Do you ever get the feeling that what you are eating is just not satisfying?

I had been eating cereal or oatmeal for breakfast most mornings, but felt I just needed something else to feel full/satisfied. Knowing we should always listen to our bodies, I have recently added a glass of skim milk and toast.

We found a study conducted by the University of Sydney in Australia. They gave each food a numerical "satisfaction" rating. The higher the rating, the longer you have the feeling of being full. Here are their numbers... "vellie intewestin..." to say the least!

Food	Rating
Potatoes	323
Fish	225
Oatmeal	209
Oranges	202
Apples	197
Whole-wheat pasta	188
Steak	176
Baked beans	168
Grapes	162
Grain bread	154
Popcorn	154
Bran Cereal	151
Eggs	150
Cheese	146
White rice	138
Lentils	133
Brown rice	132
Crackers	127

White pasta	119
Bananas	118
White bread	100

That good old potato (that has often gotten such a bad rap) is on top of the list in satisfaction! I also thought it interesting they found white rice was more satisfying (but very little more) than brown rice.

Being able to control how much we eat is high on our priority list in a successful weight loss program. And, staying satisfied for a longer period of time is **the** key to keeping us from overeating. Give this research list your serious consideration.

50. Attention Chocoholics! Think you can't lose weight and satisy your "addiction" at the same time? Better take a close look at this secret!

What wonderful, surely sinful indulgence have you eliminated from your weight loss program? Perchance it might be chocolate?

Everything I have picked up lately was talking about the benefits of chocolate. We all shy away from it because of the high level of saturated fat in chocolate due to the presence of cocoa butter, which increases blood cholesterol levels.

Also, we have been discouraged because of the high caffeine level. A regular cup of coffee contains from ninety to one hundred fifty milligrams of caffeine whereas a one ounce piece of chocolate contains only 25 milligrams. Hey maybe if you are watching your caffeine intact a little less coffee and a piece of that forbidden fruit... chocolate.

In a study by Holland's National Institute of Public Health and Environment, chocolate was found to have four times the antioxidants of green tea. The institute further states that chocolate also provides endorphins, which act like natural opiates in treating chronic pain.

Endorphins also bring on a relaxed state of mind, enable more oxygen to reach our inner blood supply and even improve our memory. Seratonin, a neurotransmitter is found in chocolate and works in our body as an anti-depressant.

When we are stressed out and little depressed about not having some favorite food such as chocolate, that old feeling of deprivation creeps in. So if you can eat a small amount of chocolate without overdoing it, why not incorporate a small amount into your weight loss program.

The sugar free/fat free frozen chocolate bars or fat free cocoa mixes will still give you the same antioxidant benefit without the calories. Dark chocolate is more effective than milk chocolate. The more expensive the chocolate, the better for you.

51. How you can easily enjoy your favorite calorie rich salad dressing without adding calories to your diet. This is one of the neatest tricks we've seen!

Always put your salad dressing into a small bowl and dip your fork into it before each bite of your salad. You'll get the taste of the dressing that you are really craving. You will also consume much less dressing and will save those extra calories. When you eat at a restaurant, always ask for your salad dressing "on the side."

52. Here is an item from your supermarket that will make your favorite recipes absolutely delicious... "finger licking good" without adding fat or calories.

Swanson Chicken Broth put out by Campbell Soup Company is a great way to "cut the fat" in your recipes...

and at the same time, make them "finger licking good." It adds zero fat and only a couple of calories per serving.

Try the Seasoned Chicken Broths such as Roasted Garlic and Italian Herbs in your favorite recipes. No butter necessary.

Swanson advertises the "Skinny Mashed Potatoes." These too can be seasoned with just the plain Swanson Chicken Broth or you can be creative by trying one of the Seasoned Broths. Swanson has recently added "Seasoned Chicken Broth with Roasted Garlic" and "Seasoned Chicken Broth with Italian Herbs" to their line of broths.

You can even use the Swanson's Chicken Broth in your favorite dressing recipe.

Swanson's fat free broths are the best thing since sliced bread. It has so many uses for flavoring your foods without adding fat.

You can substitute one of these tasty fat-free broths for water when cooking rice or pasta and eliminate the need for butter or salt.

You can use also use them for basting chicken, pork, or fish during cooking.

You can even use them to moisten leftovers such as turkey, chicken, pork, or even casseroles before reheating.

What a great way to flavor your meals and cut those calories! A bonus is that the taste is sooooo good!

53. How to always get the best salad greens and save money at the same time.

Buy precut salad greens. You are able to get a greater variety in your salads. Plus, they are much less expensive than buying several types of lettuce that will go bad before you can possibly eat them up.

54. Use this neat little "doggie bag" trick to cut the calories and save you money when eating in a restaurant.

If you receive large portions when eating in a restaurant, always ask for a doggie bag at the **beginning** of the meal. Place the portions that you know you shouldn't eat in the carryout before you start eating. This will make an excellent "TV" dinner for you on another day and you will not be tempted to overeat.

55. How to use the microwave at work to prepare quick, low-calorie, but delicious lunches.

Quick Lunch: Take a sweet or white potato to work. Most places have a microwave and refrigerator. Top the white potato with fat free sour cream and add a little cinnamon or nutmeg to the sweet potato.

Also, don't forget that Weight Watchers, Lean Cuisine, and Healthy Choice offer delicious low calorie and low fat meals at your local supermarket that you can microwave.

56. How to use egg-substitutes to lower your calorie intake... even if you don't like egg-substitutes.

Recipes: Be creative in the kitchen. Try your favorite recipes substituting low fat and low sugar.

Most new recipes have a nutrition count printed at the bottom. This is most helpful in calculating the portions for the recipe.

Egg substitutes definitely lower calories. Many of us do not like the egg substitutes as a main course for breakfast. In other cooking, however, you can't tell a difference in taste from the real thing. Even at breakfast, the egg substitutes are delicious in an omelet when mixed with a little fat free cheese, lean ham and spices and can make a great meal! Try it... you'll like it.

57. How to use the fact that cats eat many mini-meals and cattle graze to help you lose weight.

Have you ever noticed how cats eat lots of mini-meals each day and how cattle graze? They spend their days nibbling. We humans have become so conscious of NOT snacking that we tend to over-eat when we do sit down for a meal.

More and more nutritionists are recommending we eat smaller amounts more frequently. It really makes sense to eat smaller portions. This will keep the old tummy from stretching to accommodate the food intake. It may even keep your tummy from showing through your dress or shirt so prominently. :-)

Snacking on good healthy foods such as fruits, veggies, popcorn, a bowl of soup, or even a little peanut butter on a couple of crackers between meals will help prevent us from stuffing at meal time.

So keep good healthy snacks handy for those in-between-times and "quelch" that hunger before it starts.

58. How one of Lillie's readers lost 40 pounds and a significant number of points off his blood pressure with Souper Soup.

One of our readers followed the Souper Soup plan for the week and lost seven pounds. He liked the soup so well that he still has a bowl of it as one of his meals each day. (He also eats two balanced meals--- which makes this safe.) This is also a good way to get your "Five or More" Veggies for the day.

Ron says he eats a **sweet potato** each day as we advise in an another "Secret." This is a "most important" food in fighting fat. Please consider it in your personal weight loss plan.

Ron tells us, "Being lucky enough to live in Florida, I am able to go for a 5 mile bike ride almost every morning. This is a super way to exercise and never gets boring." He says he **"has now lost 40 pounds and has taken a significant number of points off his blood pressure reading."** He has reached his weight goal... in fact he is 10 pounds below it.

Ron is still eating a bowl of Souper Soup every day.

WOW! What **great** results! Thanks Ron for sharing this with us!

Incidentally... don't tell Ron I told ya... but he is 69 years young which makes this doubly amazing.

Anyone else out there who wants to eat a bowl of Souper Soup plus a sweet potato and ride your bike every day? **You can do it too, my friend... and reach your weight goal!**

59. Here are 16 fun and delicious treats you'll love because they add only 100 calories.

100-Calorie Fun Things to Eat

2 1/2 Miniature candy bars (Snickers, Milky Way etc.)
1/2 A Hershey bar
1/2 Reese's Peanut Butter Cup

23 Chocolate-covered raisins
1 Fudgsicle
1 Haagen-Dazs Raspberry Vanilla Ice Cream Bar
1 Popsicle
1 Homemade chocolate or oatmeal chip cookie
1 Betty Crocker Sweet Rewards bar
5 Gingersnaps
1/2 Small order of French Fries
4 Cups of light popcorn
2 Tablespoons of Cashews
2 Tablespoons of Smucker's Guilt-free Hot Fudge
1/4 Cup of premium ice cream
1/2 Cup low-fat ice cream or frozen yogurt

60. Here are butter and margarine substitutes that will make your cakes light, moist and delicious while reducing calories considerably.

Want to lighten up that favorite cake or brownie recipe? Substitute fat free mayonnaise for butter and margarine. It will make your cake so moist and good--- while reducing calories considerably. Other good butter and margarine substitutes are applesauce, dried fruit purees and baby food.

The next time you need to take a cake or brownies to a get-together such as a potluck supper at church or a family reunion, try substituting the oil or fat with one of these ingredients. Mum's the word--- and no one will know that you have lightened up a favorite recipe because the good taste will still be there.

61. Lillie's Low Fat Recipe for "Wraps." Umm mm good... and yet very low in calories.

Lillie's Low Fat Recipe for "Wraps"

1 low-fat Tortilla or Pita Pocket

1 ounce of grilled chicken slices
1 slice of fat-free cheese or shredded Tofu cheese
Salad fixings (prepackaged)
Chopped Red & Yellow bell peppers
Chopped Tomato
Chopped Scallion
Hellman's Dijonaise
Salt and Pepper to taste

I use a Tortilla that is flavored with herbs. Or a Flavored Pita pocket can be used. (Such as onion) The precooked chicken is so handy to use.

I have also used the 98% fat free roast beef and ham slices. You can load on the veggies as free food. This can be as big as you want it to be with veggies, but be accurate putting the meat and cheese on the sandwich. It is sooooooo filling and sooooooo good.

Be creative!!!

62. Here are your best weight loss choices at Arby's, Boston Market, and Burger King.

When choosing to eat out at fast food places, you don't have to do the "greasy-gain-a-pound" scene. Here are some better choices you can make at the various quickie servers.

ARBY'S
Light Grilled Chicken Salad	190 calories
Light Roast Chicken Salad	200 calories
Light Roast Chicken Deluxe	260 calories
Light Grilled Chicken	280 calories

BOSTON MARKET
Skinless Rotisserie Turkey Breast	170 calories
Meat Loaf and Chunky Tomato Sauce	370 calories
Southwest Savory Chicken	400 calories
Ham Sandwich (no cheese or sauce)	440 calories

BURGER KING
Chicken Tenders (4 pieces)	180 calories
Hamburger	320 calories
Cheeseburger	360 calories
BK Broiler Sandwich (no mayo)	370 calories

63. Here's a banana recipe... guaranteed to taste yummy good... and yet help you take off pounds and inches.

Do you remember Mom freezing bananas when you were a kid? They are so tasty and good. You can spread a little honey on them and add a few sprinkles such as nuts and graham cracker crumbs.

Don't dip them... just sprinkle and the calories are minimal. . Put a craft stick in them and they are so goooooood and coooooling.

64. How to lower the calories and fat in your favorite Cajun dishes.

Rice and beans are such good high fiber foods and there are so many ways you can flavor them.

The Cajuns in Louisiana serve a delicious red beans and rice dish on Mondays. Their recipes usually call for adding a spicy sausage to the beans and rice. You can lower the calories in these by using low fat ham or turkey sausage.

As always, be creative in the kitchen. (You were before you started to lose weight weren't you?)

65. More "better choices" when you eat out at Dunkin Donuts, Hardee's, or McDonalds.

DUNKIN' DONUTS

Bran Muffin	240 calories
Cranberry Orange, Low fat	240 calories
Banana or Blue Berry, Low fat	250 calories
Low Fat Chocolate	250 calories

HARDEE'S

Hamburger	270 calories
Hot Ham 'N' Cheese	300 calories
Regular Roast Beef	310 calories
Grilled Chicken Sandwich	350 calories

McDONALD'S

Grilled Chicken Salad Dlx... (w/o dressing)	120 calories
Chicken McNuggets (4 pieces)	190 calories
English Muffin	140 calories
Egg McMuffin	290 calories

66. Two things to ask your waiter in a restaurant that will help you take off the pounds you want to lose.

People in general are becoming more mindful of what they are eating.

And, restaurants are becoming more attuned to meeting people's needs when it comes to weight loss efforts. So don't be afraid to ask in a restaurant to put the condiments on the side for your salad or baked potato.

Ask for grilled food instead of fried, if you don't see it on the menu. Most eating-places are very accommodating. So be brave, speak up!

67. Here are your best choices when you eat at Subway, Taco Bell or Wendy's.

SUBWAY
Veggie Delight	232 calories
Turkey Breast	282 calories
Roast Beef	296 calories
Super Subway Club	377 calories

TACO BELL
Grilled Steak Soft Taco	200 calories
Chilli Cheese Burrito	330 calories
Grilled Chicken Burrito	390 calories
Big Beef Burrito	400 calories

WENDY'S
Grilled Chicken Sandwich	310 calories
Plain Single Hamburger	360 calories
Garden Veggie-Fresh Stuffed Pita	400 calories
Spicy Chicken Sandwich	410 calories

When in doubt, ask the fast food restaurant for a nutrition chart on their foods.

68. Here's something you should try on your cereal instead of milk. It tastes better and adds fewer calories.

Cereal and Milk: The flaked type cereal is a great source of important nutrients, but it is not very filling. If you are like me, it seems to go down so very quickly. I have found the flavored low fat or no fat yogurts sweetened with artificial sweeteners on my cereal take longer to eat.

(Remember it takes twenty minutes for your tummy to know that you are full.) Cereals with the yogurt are crunchy and truly delicious.

While we are on the subject of cereals, how about oatmeal? Mom knew what she was doing when she gave it to us when we were young. It really does "stick to your ribs" and you are truly not as hungry waiting for that next meal. Try it-- You'll like it!

69. Here are some soy-based foods that are super tasty and will help you lose weight.

Tofu (Soy products): The first time I tried tofu was years ago and it was the worst ice cream I had ever eaten. My sister-in-law bought it for me, and I had to be polite and eat it. Yuck!

So when all of the new soy and tofu products came out, I was very reluctant to try them. But, one of the members of an exercise class that I attend was telling us she had found some products in the produce section of the grocery store that were delicious.

I found the soy cheeses are especially super tasty. They come in lots of flavors, such as cheddar, pepperjack and feta.

When I first started trying them, they were available only in slices like you find American cheese, but now you can also get them shredded. They are great for toppings on salads, potatoes, or in an omelet.

They melt easily. Give them a try. They truly are good--- and good for you!

70. Here is an 8-calorie dessert to satisfy your sugar cravings!

Sugar free Jell-O Gelatin has only 8 calories a serving. It makes for such an easy low calorie dessert to have on hand when you have that sugar craving.

Add some fruit and you get in one those needed "five or more" fruit servings a day.

The Jell-O puddings are only 100 calories a serving when made with skim milk.

This is great way to get part of your milk in, especially if you really don't like drinking that glass of milk you know you need.

71. Here are your best weight loss choices when you eat in Asian, French, Italian or Mexican restaurants.

Dining Out: For those restaurants that are not fast food, here some good choices for lower calorie food:

Asian Foods:

Egg drop soup	180 calories
Won ton soup	180 calories
2 won tons	180 calories
Egg roll w/shrimp	190 calories
Chow mein with shrimp	260 calories***
Beef teriyaki	335 calories***
Chicken teriyaki	355 calories***
Sweet & Sour Pork	480 calories***

*** Serving size of 1 1/2 to 2 cups includes rice and are used for the main course.

French Foods:

Beef Burgundy	350 calories***
Chicken Cordon Bleu	390 calories***
Spinach Crepe	520 calories***

*** Serving size of 1 1/2 to 2 cups and should be used for a main course. Include a salad and low fat or no fat dressing. Watch your calories at your other meals for the day.

Italian Foods:

Linguini w/scallops	276 calories***
Linguini w/ shrimp	288 calories***
Chicken primavera	360 calories***

Fettuccini Alfredo w/shrimp   367 calories***
Lasagna 428 calories***

*** Serving size approximately 1 1/2 to 2 cups. Remember to make these a main course and add a salad on the side with low fat or no-fat dressing. You might bring your own dressing.

Mexican Foods:

Chicken Fajita   226 calories***
Taco   230 calories***
Tostada   240 calories***
Chicken Enchilada   310 calories***
Chilli w/beans   330 calories***
Taco Salad w/ salad   380 calories***

*** Serving size approximately 1 1/2 to 2 cups. Use as a main course.

72. Here are your best choices to help you lose weight when you eat at Taco Bell, Wendy's, Arby's, Burger King, Hardee's, KFC, McDonalds, Subway, or Pizza Hut. Some of these will absolutely amaze you how low they are in calories!

Taco Bell Taco   170 calories
Wendy's Caesar Salad   100 calories
Arby's Roast Beef sandwich deluxe   296 calories
Burger King Side salad with dressing   240 calories
Hardee's Hamburger   270 calories
KFC Roast Chicken Breast w/skin   251 calories
McDonald's Grilled Chicken salad   120 calories
Subway Club on white bread   297 calories
Pizza Hut Veggie Lover's Thin'N Crispy 222 calories*

* Based on 1/6 of a medium pizza and 1/8 of a large pizza

Remember if you add condiments such as mayonnaise to the sandwiches, the calorie count will change. Mustard and catsup are much lower in calories (only 15 calories per serving.) Regular mayonnaise has 100 calories per tablespoon.

73. A delicious beverage that automatically burns about 450 calories per week without effort on your part! An added bonus... it may reduce heart attack and cancer risk!

Consider drinking Green Tea to help you lose weight. If you just really hate the taste of tea, then go to your local health food store and ask for Green Tea Extract.

Recent studies by The Mayo Clinic show that six to eight cups of Green Tea daily--- or the extract equivalent--- automatically burns about 450 calories per week for a female on a diet of 1600 calories per day.

We're talking "effortless" calorie burning here! Researchers think that Green Tea promotes the burning of fat because it contains substances called catechins.

Drinking Green Tea offers an added bonus of reducing heart attack and cancer risk! Try it. You'll probably like it!!

74. Here's an easy way to quickly "measure" servings when eating out or grocery shopping.

Don't have that scale with you when eating out or grocery shopping?

Oh, but you have the next best thing? Your **hand**!

A clinched fist is the approximate size of a piece of fruit such as an apple, orange or pear. Stretch your fingers and the distance from the tip of your little finger to your thumb is just about the size a banana should be.

Make a fist with your fingers up--- and that's about a half-cup or a side dish serving of pasta, rice, or some other type grain. If the serving is the main course double it for a whole cup.

75. Foods you should never keep in your home. Always go out to eat them.

It is very hard to keep things like ice cream or frozen yogurt or cookies in the house when you are trying to lose weight.

So make it a **special occasion** to go out to your favorite ice cream or yogurt shop. Order the child's portion of ice cream or yogurt in a cup.

Sit down and really enjoy each bite. Take the same time to eat as you would for a meal... 15 to 20 minutes. Really taste it. Don't just wolf it down.

Most malls have a bakery. Get two cookies if you are a "cookieholic" like me and go find a bench and do the same thing with cookies. Maybe add a cup of tea or coffee to go with it.

Make these goodies--- **treats**. Treats like Mom gave you or you have given your children when they have been good.

76. Use this secret and add nuts to your weight loss program without gaining weight.

Nuts: To partake or not to partake. I have found my biggest problem with eating nuts is knowing when to stop eating them.

As a child, I can remember the excitement of getting nuts at Christmas. And my very favorites were English walnuts.

The reason they were such a favorite, besides their wonderful taste, was probably the fact that I could get into them so easily... much easier than pecans.

I have always purchased my walnuts at the local grocery store, but this last weekend a friend of mine returned from California. His daughter had walnut trees in her yard and he had picked me a huge sack full. What a wonderful present. I had never had fresh picked English walnuts!

On weight loss programs, we have a tendency to steer away from nuts, but they are such a healthy snack. 80% of the fat in walnuts is mono- or polyunsaturated and walnuts are a good source of Omega-3 fatty acids.

Including a few walnuts in your holiday treats can help lower your risk of coronary heart disease. A serving size is 1/4 cup. It seems like such a small amount. There are 210 calories in 1/4 cup of walnuts. **But**... if you sprinkle some chopped nuts on your hot cereal in the morning, you may only need a teaspoon or so. They will go a long way.

Another way is to mix 1/4 cup with hot air pop corn. Or add a few to your fresh fruit or yogurt. Also, a few scattered in your fresh green salad will add so much flavor. I recommend using the nuts that have not been roasted and salted.

Nuts are so good for you! They are a good source of fiber.

Eating them by the hand full is where you get into trouble! Measure them out and put the rest back "out of sight and out of mind." Enjoy!

For information about this wonderful nut, check out **California Walnuts** at http://www.walnut.org

77. How you can keep from falling for the weight gain "sugar-free" and "fat-free" tricks food companies use on their labels.

Let's face it folks. The thing that people who make fat free and sugar free products have to accomplish is to make them **taste good**.

In order to accomplish this, they sometimes add fat to the sugar free products and sugar to the fat free products. You know how we love the taste of fat and sugar! However, what happens often is there are loads of calories in these products.

A calorie is a calorie is a calorie anyway you look at it. And, **calories count** when you are trying to lose weight.

Watch the nutrition labels on these products. Even though they say fat free and sugar free they are not necessarily **calorie free**.

78. Here's an easy way you can save a bundle of money while you lose weight.

Did you know that you don't have to buy the high-priced, low-fat cooking sprays? You can easily make your own for pennies!

Buy a low-cost, non-aerosol spray bottle in house wares in your favorite department store or Walmart, Kmart, etc. You may even find them in house wares at the grocery store. And, all you have to do is add your favorite extra-virgin olive oil and spray away.

You can spray your pans before cooking or spray onto your foods such as salads or veggies. You can spray your meat before grilling. It's a big calorie and money saver.

If you mix a little olive oil into one of the flavored vinaigrettes, you can make your own spray for your salads. Saves scads of calories as opposed to drowning them with dressing--- and it tastes great!

79. Here is a collection of free recipes... worth more than the combined price of half a dozen of the cookbooks you buy in your book store!

Don't you just love getting **good** things free?

Equal Sweetener has a newsletter that you can subscribe to free... and get free recipes that are absolutely delicious while at the same time being low calorie and low or no fat.

It has wonderful recipes made with Equal. Also, the recipes include nutrition information. These recipes are on cards that can be detached and put in your recipe file.

There are wonderful tips on preparing food with Equal. Also, there other tips on preparing other foods in low calorie ways.

You'll also get a free Equal Sweetener Conversion Chart to help you figure out just how much Equal to use in your own favorite recipe.

To receive this newsletter visit **Equal Sweetener** at http://www.equal.com

They will also give you free coupons for money saving offers of Equal.

80. How you can easily reduce the fat in a can of tuna.

I get caught up eating the same old thing sometimes. And-- forget about some old tips and foods that I used to enjoy eating. So I thought I would bring back a few.

I like tuna fish salad, but all the mayo adds calories. Also, a lot of tuna is packed in oil.

However, if you drain the Tuna in a colander and then rinse it with hot water from the tap you will get rid of a lot of the fat. (The oil packed is cheaper.) However, if you don't want to use the tuna packed in oil, get the tuna packed in water.

Cut down on the mayonnaise calories by adding a little mustard to taste and use low fat or no fat mayo. An apple cut up will extend the amount of salad and will give it a really good taste.

81. Here's a turkey buying trick to save you half the money you'd ordinarily spend... and yet get a meal with only half the calories.

When you are getting ready to purchase your Thanksgiving and Christmas Turkeys, consider buying the breast instead of the whole turkey. The calories are much lower. You may very well spend only half the money and get less than half as many calories.

Use chicken broth to make your corn bread dressing instead of the turkey drippings.

Also use the broth in your mashed potatoes. Swanson Chicken Broth gives you a good recipe on the can for "skinny" mashed potatoes

When making your green bean casserole for Thanksgiving, remember that Campbell's Soups make fat free soups such as Cream of Mushroom.

Get those recipes out and start getting ready for Thanksgiving and Christmas, so that you can have a guilt free day.

82. What to look for in your local farmer's market or roadside produce stand to help you lose weight.

While we were on vacation, I noticed all of the produce stands along the road.

The Fall is a great time of the year to get all those healthy foods at their peak in flavor.

Sweet potatoes are so high in beta-carotene, fiber and vitamin C. And they taste so good. (Don't cover them up with butter or margarine!) Use the spray butter instead.

Apples are plentiful--- and so good for you. They come in such a variety of types.

If you live in the South, the greens such as mustard, turnips and collards are plentiful in the Fall. But don't dare add that "fat back" like Grandma did.

So get out and find your Farmers Market, or take a ride in country and partake of these good healthy foods.

83. Here are delicious low cost, yet healthy dishes guaranteed to take off the pounds you want to lose!

In the late Fall... and leafy greens are definitely available in abundance. Best sources are farmers markets and/or local produce stands. If these sources are unavailable in your area... Kroger, Safeway or Winn Dixie usually offer a great selection.

In the South, Turnips, Mustard, and Collards are at their best in the Fall. In other parts of the U.S., Escarole, Broccoli Raab, Spinach, and Kale are readily available and can easily be prepared to be super tasty.

Leafy greens fill your tummy with scads of fiber and eliminate hunger pangs, while contributing very few calories to your diet. They also supply scads of valuable vitamins and minerals. For us females, the iron they contribute to our diet is the very best available.

Prepare leafy greens by washing and trimming them to eliminate the tough stems. Cover with water and cook over a low to medium heat until they are tender. Greens taste much better when you flavor them with a little chicken or beef broth along with your favorite herbs.

84. Here are little-known facts on the food rated as the number one fat fighter... and at the same time a major cancer fighter! Better yet... it's delicious!!!

Sweet potatoes have been rated by several tests as the number one food that fights fat. The complex-carbohydrates and fiber they contain satisfies your appetite and helps regulate your blood sugar levels.

A huge bonus is that sweet potatoes contain scads of vitamin A that is known to be a major cancer cell fighter.

Sweet potatoes are easy to prepare. Bake them in your oven at 325 - 350 degrees for 45 to 55 minutes. You can also wrap them in foil and grill them for a comparable time. Quicker yet is to pierce them with a fork several times and microwave them on your high temperature setting for about 7 minutes per average size potato.

Flavor your sweet potatoes with a little cinnamon and/or nutmeg to taste. Better yet, a small bit of Lite "I Can't Believe It's Not Butter" spray margarine will make them a real weight-loss taste treat!

85. The little-known secret why you see very few overweight people in China. NO... it is not because they don't get enough to eat! Use this tidbit to quickly and easily take off pounds and inches... look better and feel better.

How do the Chinese do it? Have you been to China lately? If you've strolled the streets of modern day Beijing, Shanghai or Hong Kong--- you have surely noticed the **very** low number of overweight people.

This lack of fat folks is even very apparent on the television news channel shots from these cities.

No--- it has nothing to do with the Chinese not having enough to eat. Believe me, here in the twenty first century, these folks are well fed. Their "hunger" level is probably less than here in the U.S., or the U.K, and other Western nations!

The primary reason the Chinese have few overweight people is due to the major ingredient of their diet being RICE. No, not the pretty super-white, "polished" processed rice which is most often served in the U.S. The nucleus of the Chinese diet is unpolished BROWN rice.

Try it... and you'll like it. The chewy texture will slow down your shoveling in the next bite, while at the same time, it will fill you up with fiber.

Our personal favorite for a quick source is 10 minute Success Brown Rice distributed by Riviana Foods, Inc. in Houston Texas. An average serving is one cup of prepared rice. That will only add 150 measly calories to your diet.

Season the rice to your taste with salt, pepper or the herbs of your choice. A tad of Lite "I Can't Believe It's Not Butter" margarine won't hurt your weight-loss efforts--- but will add a lot to the taste of your rice.

If you want to really "do it up brown," add a couple tablespoons of Heinz Home Style Savory Beef Gravy to your rice. It tastes great, but will only add about 3 to 5 calories to the 150 of your cup of prepared brown rice!

86. Craving sugar-laden cookies and cakes? Here's how you can satisfy that craving with delicious supermarket items... with no sugar, no fat and less cost.

Try making a meal of tropical fruits. Pineapple, mangoes, kiwi and papaya help you lose weight while supplying a buttery sweet flavor with absolutely no fat.

These tropical goodies will also satisfy your craving for deserts such as sugar laden cookies and cakes.

Better yet, these fruits are a super source of vitamins, minerals, and fiber.

Go to your supermarket and try to get fruit that is completely ripe. Cut them up and serve chilled as a salad.

87. How to choose a low calorie, low fat salad. Some available at well known places weigh in at nearly 700 calories and 50 grams of fat!

Doesn't salad just say "diet food?" It IS a great source of veggies and it IS an excellent addition to any meal. You can even make a complete meal on a salad.

However, we need to watch out for some types of salads. Caesar salad dressings can be loaded with calories. I found one chicken Caesar salad with a whopping 670 calories and 47 grams of fat.

Also there were 590 calories and 30 grams of fat in a Taco Salad from one fast food restaurant.

You could have a hamburger for fewer calories and fat. A double hamburger plain at Wendy's has 560 calories and 29 grams of fat.

A garden salad or side salads are usually just veggies and you add your own dressing. These truly are low calorie salads.

So, don't kid yourself that having just any kind of salad is a low calorie meal. Ask for calorie counts. Most places will be glad to let you know which are the lower calorie meals.

88. How to enjoy holiday parties without blowing your weight loss plan.

Parties during the holidays can be a real challenge for someone trying to lose weight. Two things are important about going to parties. One is the food and the other is what to wear?

Never go to a party hungry. Before leaving for the party, always have something to eat that is on your food program.

At the party, have a non-alcoholic drink such as a virgin Bloody Mary. Specialty waters with a twist of lime and lemon are also great. A cup of coffee is another sipper you can have.

I feel that most people are getting weight and nutrition conscious and there is usually something low calorie that you can find to eat at any party.

The problem is those foods that we can not stop with eating just one.

One thing that is helpful in these situations is to offer to bring a recipe that is low calorie, low fat. Get out those cookbooks and substitute applesauce for butter in those cake recipes. Be creative.

Find someone to talk to that you haven't seen since a party last year. Get a cup of coffee... and sip and visit. Don't linger near the food table!

89. Here's a wonderful new convenient, (and great tasting) way to buy tuna fish.

Tuna has been a "staple" in our weight loss regimen for a long time. It tastes great--- it's low fat, low cholesterol, low calorie--- and you can serve it many different ways.

While buying Christmas dinner items, I happened upon a wonderful new and convenient way to buy tuna fish.

Star Kist is now packaging tuna in a handy foil, no drain package. I picked up a sample package of the "chunk light."

It has only 60 calories and .5g of fat for a 2 oz. serving. It also comes in Albacore and chunk light packed in sunflower oil.

What a great item to pack for lunch! You don't have to drain it. You don't need a can opener to get into it, and the regular size package makes up to four sandwiches!

Put some whole wheat bread, light mayo or mustard in you lunch box, and make yourself a great tuna sandwich for lunch.

Now, you can also find salmon as well as chicken in the same handy foil packets. Try it... you'll like it!

90. How to add sex appeal (and super taste) to a boring lettuce salad.

Lettuce alone is such a boring salad. I went to a banquet recently where the salad they served consisted of only lettuce, with a just hint of red cabbage and carrot.

There are lots of greens that can be added to a salad to give it color and taste. Consider spinach, arugla, chicory, collards, dandelion greens, kale, mustard greens, Swiss chard and watercress. Many prepackaged salad fixings have these greens in them.

Consider adding grated vegetables to your recipes. The Mayo Clinic Health Letter suggests adding grated carrots, potatoes and apples to lean ground beef and turkey, when making meat loaf and meat balls. This makes for a moisturizing filler in these recipes.

I always add apple to my tuna salad. It makes it go farther and it tastes so good.

91. Here's a tuna recipe you're going to love. Tastes great and is only 240 calories per serving.

For lunch today I found a recipe on the back of the new foil packed StarKist Tuna for "Tuna Meltaways."

The ingredients are:

1 - 7 oz. package StarKist Tuna
2 cups shredded cheddar cheese
1/2 cup finely chopped celery
1/2 cup finely chopped onion
1/2 cup shredded carrot
2 Tbs. light mayonnaise
6 English muffins split

Directions: Heat broiler. In medium bowl combine all ingredients except muffins; mix well. Divide tuna mixture evenly onto muffin halves. Place on broiler pan; broil 4 to 6 inches from heat 6 to 8 minutes or until lightly browned and bubbly. Serve warm.

They were delicious. My husband, who doesn't usually like tuna, admitted they were good.

Instead of regular cheddar cheese, I use shredded pepper jack & cheddar soy cheese or one of the fat free cheeses.

The tuna has only 70 calories a serving. The English muffins I used had 120 calories for the whole muffin. The mayonnaise had 50 calories for the whole recipe.

The veggies, of course, are "free food." You will have to calculate for yourself to be exact. But, as you can see, this makes a very low calorie quick lunch--- and it really tastes good too.

92. How the timing of something as simple as brushing your teeth can help you lose weight!

Our reader Therese, says she brushes her teeth immediately after eating and it deters that urge to eat more. Add flossing and mouth wash and your dentist will love you when you go for your next checkup. And, the bonus is--- you will be a thinner you!

Another tip a reader shared is eating grapefruit in the morning.

As Toni said, you need to like grapefruit. The best type Toni found comes in a seal packed jar. It's already peeled--- all the work is done for you.

I have never really liked grapefruit, but I have tried it and have found that I am more satisfied. My taste for grapefruit is definitely changing.

And, the bonus is that you have eaten another one of those five or more fruits and/or veggies a day.

A note of warning however... we're told that people on certain prescription drugs should not eat grapefruit. You'll want to check on this before adding them to your diet.

93. Lillie's personal recipe for scrumptious low fat, low calorie breakfast muffins.

Several people have requested a recipe for low fat muffins--- for breakfast or a snack.

I like using my own favorite recipe and modify it to make it low fat.

My personal favorite is Refrigerator Bran Muffins. This makes a large quantity of muffins and the mix will keep for weeks in the refrigerator.

All you have to do is preheat the oven before you take that morning shower and pop in one or the number needed for your family to have a hot, healthy breakfast.

You can bake them all at once, freeze them, and zap in the microwave as needed.

However, it sure is nice to have the smell of fresh baked muffins in your home! By making them as needed there are no leftovers to tempt you. And, they are always fresh.

The recipe:

1 (15 oz.) box Raisin Bran
5 tsp. soda
5 cups flour
1 tsp. cloves
2 tsp. salt
1 tsp. cinnamon
Egg substitute equal to 4 eggs

1/2 cup of oil
1 quart of low fat buttermilk
1/2 cup of applesauce
3 cups sugar
2 tsp. vanilla 1 tsp. nutmeg

Mix bran, sugar, flour, soda, salt, and spices in extra large bowl. Add eggs, oil, applesauce, buttermilk, and vanilla. Mix well. Store in covered container. Bake in muffin pan for 15 minutes in 400 degree oven.

1 muffin is a serving.

By using egg substitute and applesauce you greatly cut the fat content. I haven't tried sugar substitute, but this too might be an option. Also, get the low fat buttermilk. There is a difference in it and regular buttermilk.

If you don't want to make them from scratch, Krusteaz Brand makes wonderful fat-free muffin mixes. My favorites are Cranberry Orange and Wild Blueberry. Duncan Hines has a Kellogg's All-Bran Apple Cinnamon muffin mix that is also very low fat and low calorie.

Most muffins fixed this way are from 130 to 160 calories, 5 grams of fat, and 3 grams of fiber per muffin. This may vary a little, depending on what products you use. Always read your labels.

Several folks have said they don't like raisins. No problem. You can substitute bran flakes or all bran.

94. How the color of your plate may affect your appetite.

Mona says "I've heard that it helps to eat on blue plates, as that is not commonly a color associated with food."

In keeping with this, have you noticed how many restaurants have a "red" decor? The color red is supposed to stimulate your appetite. Use these "color" theories to your advantage!

95. How a cup of bouillon can make you "feel like you're cheating," but you're really not.

Granmum says that on a cold wintry day she enjoys a cup of bouillon. "It makes you feel like you are cheating... but you are not."

(Also, there are a lot of low fat, sugar-free hot chocolate mixes that are very low calorie. Add a dollop of fat free whipped topping such as Cool Whip and you have a great afternoon snack. It also makes a great dessert.)

Another tip for those people counting calories was sent to us by Franklin. He uses a grocery store clicker to count his calories.

Joan said her daughter had lost weight by eating only when she is hungry and eating what she likes in small amounts. And, she has kept the weight off doing this.

Beverly says, "If you really feel you have to have something--- or you will be deprived and eat 4 "somethings" in its place--- eat a little but keep the portion small."

96. Here are some wonderful potato recipes to help you lose weight.

Would you please pass the potatoes? To indulge, or not to indulge in potatoes during a weight loss program?

Did you know that potatoes have fewer calories than a lot of the typical so called "diet" foods?

A medium sized potato that weighs 5 ounces, which you have baked, boiled or steamed, has only 100 calories. Eight ounces of orange juice has 110 calories. One half cup of cottage cheese has 130 calories. A three-ounce hamburger has 270 calories.

It's all those "things" we add to this... one of the healthiest foods we can eat, that cause the problems. Those "things" like butter and sour cream... chilli and cheese toppings... or cooking methods such as frying absolutely destroy a successful weight loss program.

If eaten with spices and herbs that add no calories, or with a low-calorie dressing, a potato can not only be delicious, but it is so nutritious. They have zero fat grams and are high in fiber... especially if you eat the skin. They also contain vitamin C. The amount depends on the age of the potato. The newer the potato, the higher vitamin C content.

Speaking of "tasty"--- here is a very tasty low-fat, low calorie recipe for you. For a very filling, quick meal, bake a white potato, cut it in half and top with low-fat turkey chilli, fat-free sour cream and soy grated cheese. It is delicious.

Linda and Cindy add their favorite salsa on baked potatoes. Linda also said to read the ingredients on the jar since some may contain oil.

Cindy said, "A friend turned me on to a baked potato with low fat ranch dressing - as good as sour cream, I think."

Someone else suggested that a little buttermilk was just as good on a baked potato as sour cream... and so much better for the person trying to lose weight.

Potatoes are also very filling and satisfying. In fact, they are rated by researchers as the number one most satisfying food. So, order that potato the next time you go out, but don't drown it in butter and/or sour cream.

97. Learn why cabbage can be one of your best friends on any weight loss plan, and how to cook it to your best weight loss advantage.

Consider making cabbage a staple in your weight loss program.

Originating in Europe and Asia, cabbage is one of the oldest cultivated vegetables. The ancient Romans highly regarded the humble cabbage and Cato applauded its "medicinal values."

There is a large variety of cabbages... green, Savoy, bok choy, Chinese and celery cabbage. There are also many cabbage "relatives" such as Brussels sprouts, cauliflower, collard greens and broccoli.

People in the United States often reject the idea of cabbage, because of the smell when cooking and the gas producing factors that are the result of its high-fiber content.

You can easily reduce the "gassiness" of cabbage by first parboiling for 5 minutes, discard the water, rinse the cabbage and then finish cooking it in fresh water. To get maximum nutrients, you will probably do better, however, to steam your cabbage.

Our reader, Joyce has a great tip for a problem that a lot of us have with eating cabbage. She writes:

"Something I learned over 50 years ago, was to steam cabbage in about 1 cup of milk to eliminate the gas reaction. My father had an ulcer, loved cooked cabbage but couldn't eat it because of the gas.

My home-economics teacher taught us to cook cabbage in milk. The first time I did this at home my father said no way was he going eat cabbage cooked that way. However, when the rest of the family started saying how good it was, he decided to try it.

From then on that was the only way he would eat it. He never had another problem eating cooked cabbage, one of his favorite foods."

You get your money's worth of nutrients in cabbage. It is high in vitamin C and potassium. It is also very low calorie. One cup of raw cabbage is 17 calories. Because it compacts when cooking, a cup of cooked cabbage is **only** 29 calories and zero fat.

Recently, Bryan from New Zealand told me that as a child he had eaten a plate of shredded cabbage as part of his meal. Cabbage, as I have mentioned before is so very healthy.

I asked Bryan if he put any kind of dressing on his cabbage and he replied, "No." He asked me if I ate raw veggies such as cabbage, cauliflower, etc. to which I replied, "Yes," but, we in the USA are good at masking the flavors and adding calories.

I told him that we add a little shredded cabbage to our salads of lettuce, carrots, onions, green peppers, etc. and.... top it off with salad dressings.

We, also eat raw cabbage in slaw (sometimes called Coleslaw.) The mayonnaise in slaw again adds additional calories.

Maybe we need to get back to basics of our different cultures and remember from our childhood... good healthy delicious tasting foods.

Thanks, Bryan, for making us more aware of how good foods taste in their natural state.

98. Here's an easy way you can instantly eliminate 40 calories and 4.5 grams of fat from a slice of pizza just before you eat it. No change in taste!

There used to be an old commercial for men's hair cream that said, "A little dab will do you." You might apply this to eating pizza. If you use a napkin to dab the grease off of two slices of pizza, you will eliminate about a teaspoon of oil, which is 40 calories and 4.5g fat.

99. A trick that will allow you to always have low-fat, low-calorie salad dressing no matter where you eat.

When it comes to salad dressings, use low-fat, low calorie dressings or maybe a red wine vinegar. I have a friend, who carries a small plastic container of pre-measured low-fat, low-calorie dressing from home. That way she is sure of getting the right amount and kind. Also, she takes her margarine the same way. A great tip.

100. Menu terms you should always avoid when dining out.

I don't know about you, but sometimes I get tired of my own cooking, or there is a special occasion and I find myself eating out. Or, maybe because of work you have to eat out often.

There are many clues we can follow to healthy and lower calorie dining out. One of the first things to look for are cooking expressions... some good and some bad.

Look on the menu for baked, broiled (without the butter) grilled, poached, roasted, and steamed. All good.

The terms to avoid are a'la king, au gratin, basted, breaded, buttered, broasted, creamed, fricasseed or fried.

The terms sautéed or stir-fried need a few questions asked of your waiter. Ask how it is cooked. And, if it is cooked in heavy oil... avoid it. If they cook it in a small amount of oil, broth or water... this is probably OK.

Another thing to remember is to order things like salad dressing, mayo, sour cream, gravies and sauces "on the side." Partake sparingly! Take only one serving of bread, then move or get rid of the bread basket.

Avoid terms on the menu with high fat descriptions, such as fettuccine Alfredo, filet mignon with béarnaise sauce, veal parmigiana, etc.

It is certainly alright to ask that no fat be used to prepare your veggies or rice. If you don't see a light menu, ask the waiter what they offer for their lighter fare.

But above all, do not give up going out just because you are trying to lose weight.

101. Things on a help-yourself salad bar that you should avoid.

Have you ever sauntered up to a help-yourself salad bar and wondered, "What do I do next?" Do you have the idea that just because it is on the salad bar, that every thing is OK to pile on your plate?

The first things to avoid are the creamy salads such as potato, pasta and creamy coleslaw. Instead, fill your plate high with veggies such as dark leafy greens.

Don't overlook spinach. It doesn't taste like the kind cooked with eggs your mother tried to force you to eat. Load up on carrots, mushrooms, cauliflower, cucumbers, and broccoli.

Don't forget the herbs and pepper, which add taste without the sodium.

Also at the salad bar, fix yourself a plate of fruit such as fresh pineapple, melon and strawberries for dessert.

Even though they taste so good, avoid piling your plate high with things like ham, cheese, chopped eggs and pickled foods.

While at the salad bar, why not grab another plate for your entree' if it's served as a buffet. Remember the tip about using salad plates for your main course instead of a dinner plate? (You tend to put less food on them.) And, don't go back for seconds!

102. Like Coleslaw? Here is one that is fat free!

U C Berkeley Wellness Letter published a recipe for a fat free coleslaw and guess what one of main ingredients was? Apples and apple juice. It has only 74 calories for a one-cup serving. Thought you might like the recipe:

The dressing is made of:
1/2 cup plain nonfat yogurt,
3 tablespoons of apple juice and
2 tablespoons of vinegar.

This is enough for:
1 1/2 pounds of shredded cabbage with
2 cups of shredded carrots,
2 shredded celery stalks,
1/3 cup raisins, and
1 diced apple.

Nice serving size and lots of good ingredients.

103. Do you know that some beef sandwiches have less calories than the grilled chicken sandwich? Look at these fast food choices to help you lose weight.

Get ahead of the game when going to a fast food restaurant by considering the following: ca. = calories g. = grams   so. = sodium

Arby's Light grilled chicken salad	190 ca.	4 fat g.
Light roast chicken deluxe	260 ca.	5 fat g.
Light roast turkey deluxe	230 ca.	5 fat g.
Burger King BK broiler chicken sandwich	390 ca.	8 fat g.
Chicken tenders sandwich	290 ca.	10 fat g.
Chicken tenders (6 pieces)	250 ca.	14 fat g.
Hardee's Hamburger	270 ca.	11 fat g.
Grilled chicken sandwich	350 ca.	16 fat g.
Regular roast beef sandwich	310 ca.	16 fat g.
McDonald's Chicken McGrill	340 ca.	7 fat g.
Grilled chicken Caesar salad	130 ca.	2.5 fat g.
Garden Salad	130 ca.	6 fat g.
Subway 6" Seafood and crab sub	338 ca.	9 fat g
6" Cold turkey breast sub	383 ca.	4 fat g.
6" Cold veggie delite sub	232 ca.	3 fat g.

Remember that all of these are **without mayo, cheese or croutons**.

When dieting we sometimes tend to avoid beef. But, I thought it interesting that the Hardee's roast beef sandwich had fewer calories than the grilled chicken sandwich.

104. How to use beans, peas, and lentils to help you lose weight.

Several of our readers have asked me about using legumes. Legumes are part of a large family that include beans, peas and lentils.

In the bean category there are black, lima, kidney, navy and soy. Peas come in a wide variety such as black-eyed, chick peas (garbanzo beans.) and split.

For those of you who live in the Southern part of the USA there are a great number of peas such as field, crowder, lady, and purple hull.

Lentils are found in brown, pink and orange varieties.

All of these legumes are very high in protein and fiber as well as being very low calorie. Any of them can even be used as a protein source instead of meat on the days you have protein scheduled on the Souper Soup Weight Loss Plan.

If using canned instead of fresh or dry legumes, be sure to rinse well to eliminate both fat and salt used in the processing.

105. Here is a recipe for a delicious low calorie, sugar-free desert. You'll love it... especially when we tell you it has only 38 calories per serving! Pig out and have two slices (or even the whole pie) and you're still not going to gain weight!

Strawberry Pudding Gelatin Pie

1 small package vanilla sugar free cook and serve pudding.
1 small package sugar free strawberry gelatin.
4 cups sliced fresh strawberries.

Mix the pudding with 2 cups water.
Microwave according to directions for 6 minutes.
Let cool for 3 or 4 minutes.
Mix the gelatin powder into the pudding

Slice the strawberries and spread into a pie plate.
Pour the pudding, gelatin mixture over the strawberries.
(Makes a glaze)
Refrigerate for an hour.
Top with fat free or low fat whipped topping

(There is no crust.) There are 80 calories for the pudding, 40 calories for the JELL-O, and 180 calories for the strawberries. That is a total of 300 calories. If you divide the pie in six servings that's only about 50 calories a serving. And, about 38 calories a serving for eight servings. The Whipped topping... I will let you do the math on how much you top it with. :-)

One of the questions I had was how many points to allow for the pie if you're following the Weight Watchers plan. Guess what? The whole pie is only 6 points. One point per serving.

My husband is a prime example of someone who hates ANY thing that smacks of healthy or low calorie. But even he had to admit the strawberry pie is great. It is attractive and certainly doesn't seem like anything that would be low calorie. He has had a slice each day since I made it.

Enjoy!!!!!

106. Here's how to satisfy your sweet cravings without blowing your weight loss plan!

I confess......I am a "Sugarholic." I love sweets.

Forget the main course. Straight to the dessert... This is what I would like to do, but alas it just doesn't work that way. That can certainly be our downfall. If I eat anything with high sugar content, I am in BIG trouble. I want to eat the whole thing.

I am always looking for low calorie, low-fat, low-sugar or sugar-free things that satisfy this sweet tooth of mine. We have found a few to share with you.

Weight Watchers has some delicious ice cream sandwiches, that are only 2 points if you are following their program, or 130 calories and 1.5 grams of fat.

I have always liked an ice cream float. Makes me think of my teenage years. Try a scoop of vanilla frozen yogurt with a diet cola or root beer. Foamy and Yummy.

And to make strawberry short cake, I use half of a toasted English muffin with strawberries... and no fat whipped topping. The English muffin makes a delicious low calorie "short cake." The calories vary according to the brand of muffin.

A tsp. of peanut butter and one of the all fruit type jams instead of margarine on a toasted English muffin is another great treat.

Also, they have improved the taste of fat free cream cheese. Try it on your toast, bagel, or English muffin along with the all fruit jams or one of the small boxes of raisins.

I love to keep the small boxes of raisins on hand for a quick treat. Already measured out for me so I know when to stop.

And, if you are chocolate lover... Honey Maid Grahams now has chocolate ones. You get two full cracker sheets... eight pieces if you break them apart :-) They have 130 calories, 3 g of fat and 1 g of fiber. They are advertised as no cholesterol, low saturated fat and a good source of calcium.

107. How to easily get the fluid intake you need without the boredom of drinking water.

With the weather becoming warm, you may not be getting enough fluids. Fluids are so very important in any weight loss plan. And, some people have trouble drinking enough water to fulfill their fluid needs.

I love all of the herbal teas. What wonderful flavors they come in. They are naturally decaffeinated and can be used as part of your water intake.

Juices are so very convenient to use. They're certainly better for you than having a soft drink. Also, they are a great source of Vitamin C. Eating the whole fruit, however, is a much better choice for losing weight. The juices are higher in calories than a piece of the same fruits.

To make sure that I am getting all of my water for the day, I try to keep a glass or an insulated cup of water close at all times.

And remember my tip... we so often mistake hunger for thirst. Reach for some tea or water before you grab a bite to eat.

108. Use this secret to keep from blowing your weight loss plan when you dine out.

Eating out can sometimes be a problem on a weight loss program. There are things, however, you can do to help.

When you go to a restaurant where you are familiar with the menu, order from memory those lower calorie items. Don't look at the menu. It might prompt you to order a favorite that is not so low calorie.

If there is crowd, be the first one to order or let some one else place your order, and excuse yourself from the table, head for the restroom. I know from personal experience that after I hear what someone else is ordering I will change my mind and it not always what I really should have ordered!

If you are planning on a glass of wine with your meal, order it after you have ordered your food. Wine can relax our willpower and you might end up ordering more food than you planned.

Share those high calorie entrees' and desserts with someone else. This is a good way to keep from feeling deprived of those special foods that we all like so very much.

And most important of all, don't beat yourself up if you over-do a special meal out. Tomorrow is another day.

109. These vegetarian foods taste great and are very low calorie

We've had several requests from vegetarians for substitutes for the protein in our Souper Soup recipe.

You may substitute soy products or high fiber foods such as beans and peas for protein in the plan. Just don't add fats when you are cooking the beans and peas.

Soy products, beans, peas etc. are great choices for anyone on a weight loss plan... vegetarian or otherwise. High fiber foods are low in calories. There are so many soy products available now and the tastes have improved immensely over the years.

I went in Burger King the other day and they have a veggie burger available on their menu. I left off the mayo and substituted mustard and loaded it with lettuce, tomatoes, and onions... and it was good. A very low calorie meal. I feel sure other fast food places will follow suit.

There is veggie chilli available in cans. Watch those labels for sodium content. You could make a chilli burger at home with one of the veggie burgers and chilli for a special treat.

For those who are not vegetarians, keep in mind that they don't taste exactly like meat, but they are good substitutes and if dressed with condiments and fresh veggies they do make for low calorie eating.

110. Here are super delicious breakfast recipes to help you lose weight

Several readers have requested low cal, low fat breakfast ideas. We have pulled a couple of great "Smoothies" from our files that our readers have shared.

Emylie shared this one with us. She wrote, "My favorite smoothie recipe doesn't need to be exact. Put a ripe banana into the blender container, add 2 or 3 heaping tablespoons of silken tofu and about 1/4 c. orange juice. Whiz it for a moment. Add a teaspoon of vanilla flavoring and enough orange juice to make 8 oz. (At this point I always add an envelope of Equal, but it is sweet enough "as is" for some people.) Blend for a few more seconds."

Joan said (to add variety to our Souper Soup recipe) I froze a couple of the bananas and twice during the day put one in the blender along with the skim milk. Instant smoothie and it tasted delicious." Remember Day 4 has bananas and skim milk.

And from Sandra who uses Soy milk. "I make the following drink with soy milk: INGREDIENTS; Two cups of natural soy milk One banana One orange 1 tsp. ground ginger 1 tsp. flax seed 1 tsp. whey powder

Put all in blender and pulse a few seconds. A most delicious and nutritious drink. Great for an on the run breakfast. You can add your own favorite fruits.

A nurse told my husband to take a teaspoon of ginger each day because it was good for his cholesterol so I devised this drink. Also the flax seed and whey powder give us extra energy during the long winter months."

111. Use these secrets to help you stay on track during the holiday "eating season."

Thanksgiving has become the beginning of the "Eating Season." It is not over...It is just starting. And you really don't want to blow all those great efforts you have been making with your weight loss efforts. I thought a few reminders might help. You might want to copy and put in a prominent place to keep you focused on your goals.

1. Never, but never go to a party HUNGRY. Don't skip meals during the day of the party. You are setting yourself up to overeat. Eat foods within your food plan for the other meals of the day. A snack before you go will keep you from heading straight to the food table.

2. Limit the alcoholic beverages. They are high in calories. Don't you want to save them for things like sweets or maybe a special dip? Calories that is. Have some sparkling water with a twist of lime. A cup of coffee or tea is another option.

3. Offer to bring a dish. Something that you know is within your food plan. Veggie and fruit trays are a good option.

4. Avoid the food tables. You know the host/hostess has put their best foot forward in preparing the food. Find someone to talk with that you haven't seen in while. It is a great opportunity to spend time with family and friends....besides eating.

5. Allow yourself to have some treat that you especially like. Don't take and all-or-nothing attitude. It only lends to guilt.

6. And, if you feel that you have overdone it, don't take that guilt trip. Let it go. Start afresh.

7. Have fun. Enjoy. This is the season for having a great time even without eating.

112. Use these secrets to actually lose weight when you eat out at a fast food place.

We all love those fast-food places on a busy day, but here are some tips for making the trip much better.

When going for breakfast, choose things like fresh fruit, cereal, fat-free or low-fat milk... low-fat muffins or pancakes. (Some places provide sugar-free syrup for the pancakes, but in any case no butter and easy does it with the syrup.)

Order the child size burgers and fries. You will save about half the calories and two-thirds the fat. You may feel like eating more when you complete the meal, but twenty minutes later you'll be much more satisfied.

When ordering a sandwich, choose mustard rather than the mayo.

A lot of the fast food places have baked potatoes. Just don't go for those wonderful cheesy toppings.

I grant you the broccoli is low calories, but not as they serve it. Ask for the butter/margarine and dressing on the side.

Instead of those fries I mentioned above, how about a side salad instead?

Ask for a brochure on nutrition. They should be available at most fast food places.

If you really think you have to have something fried, go for the larger pieces...have a chicken breast instead of several chicken fingers. Ask for a few of the big steak fries, if available, instead of a bunch of the thin French fries. The smaller pieces absorb more of the grease. This makes for more fat and calories.

Start a collection of menus. Know what they have to offer before you get there and be the first one to order. And don't try for a five course meal. Appetizers and desserts can really add the calories.

Share servings of entrees' and desserts. Offer a taste to all, but don't partake, if they reciprocate. A big NO THANK YOU.

And when ordering a salad, don't forget my tip about the dressing. Always ask for it on the side. And dip your fork into it before taking a bite of salad. Forks don't hold much dressing, but you get that good taste without a lot of calories.

If you want to indulge in something special, choose just one indulgent food, such as dessert. And then make your other choices good, healthy, low calorie foods. Remember, depriving yourself of foods you really like can lead to overeating of something you didn't want in the first place

113. Here are the perfect snack foods when you're trying to lose weight.

Snacking is such an important part of any weight loss program. When you have the munchies it is so easy to lose sight of what we are trying to achieve and binge.

Choosing the right snacks is so essential. A small apple has only 80 calories and takes a while to eat. It is also a good source of fiber.

Don't forget the low fat microwave popcorns that are so filling. They too are good source of fiber.

When the weather is cool, try one of the low fat/sugar free cocoa mixes. It takes a while to drink them and a dollop of fat free whipped topping makes them seem like a dessert.

We have found some that have only 25 to 60 calories. Carnation Fat Free cocoa has 25 calories and Swiss Miss's Fat Free Marshmallow Lovers Cocoa has 60 calories and includes a package of miniature marshmallows.

Add another 15 calories for two tablespoons of Cool Whip Fat Free whipped topping. Oh what a great bedtime treat!

114. Use these "little extras" to help you continue to lose those pounds and inches!

One of my favorite "admissions" by one of the people in my weight loss class is so very true of a lot of us... me included.

She was very carefully checking the portion of cheese that she was allowed and found that she had cut just a little too much cheese. Instead of putting it back, she popped it into her mouth. Her mother-in-law was observing all of this and asked if she was supposed to eat the piece of cheese... Very red faced, she had to admit "no."

All those little extras we consume during the day can be a problem if we are not counting them toward our calories, points, or whatever system you are using. Those little bits and pieces of food that we don't really think about putting in our mouth may be just what is keeping you from losing.

Did you know that half of a peanut butter and jelly sandwich that your child didn't finish is a whopping 240 calories? Those little Hershey Kisses that you find on a co-workers desk are about 26 calories a piece... just 4 is 100+ extra calories. How about those fries on your husband's or child's plate that you are sneaking... those crackers and rolls you consume before your entree' comes?

Everything that goes into your mouth should be counted toward your daily totals. This is why keeping a journal or diary of some sort is so important in your weight loss program. They seem so trivial, but those little "extras" may make the difference in your losing or not losing. If you are not doing so already, please start. You may be surprised at your results.

115. Could This Be Your Perfect Snack Food?

We're often asked about a good snack food. One of the best I can think of is carrots. They have so many advantages in a weight loss plan. They taste good. Carrots can be eaten raw. Even the kids (including toddlers) like the mild tart taste of carrots.

Carrots are great to pack for a lunch on the go. They aren't messy. Carrots are readily available. They are in season all year long and inexpensive all year long. Now they come in so many ready to eat packages. I found some packaged in 3 ounce packages. (Serving size has 38 calories.) They will definitely stay fresh this way.

Carrots are low in calories. One average carrot (5 or six inches long) contains only about 20 calories. They are a great source of Beta Carotene. Beta Carotene is an antioxidant which really does help with your eye sight, heart disease, cancer and macular degeneration.

Carrots are a good source of fiber. Fiber is important to our gastrointestinal tracts and is linked to reducing cholesterol in our bodies.

I find that when I leave the real sugar alone, foods like carrots are soooo very sweet tasting. And, they are not something that will slide down in a hurry. They take a while to eat and as you know slowing down the eating is much more filling.

116. Here's how drinking a cup of a certain delicious beverage before eating can curb your appetite much cheaper, more enjoyable and much safer than any diet pill you can buy!

Our thanks to Lin for sending us the following comment about our tip on losing weight by drinking ice cold water. Other than our editor dividing her message into "bite-size" sentences and paragraphs, we have not edited it. She said it much better than we could.

Thanks Lin!

"Something to note about coffee and caffeinated tea is that caffeine is the main ingredient in diet pills. It's the main thing that cuts down on your desire to eat. The other is sugar (in the diet pills).

One cup of coffee or tea with one teaspoon of honey fifteen minutes or so before you eat is the same... as well as cheaper and more enjoyable... than taking the diet pills! You might try iced coffee or tea instead of the hot beverage and take advantage of the cold to increase calorie usage while eliminating the craving for food.

(Use this page for notes on any secrets you've found that are especially applicable to you.)

Chapter Seven

Exercise Secrets

117. How to adjust your exercise routine to the "dog days of summer."

Remember when exercising on these dog days of summer to drink plenty of water, eat light and wear light clothing. Watch those temps and try to go out in the coolest time of the day.

An air-conditioned facility, such as a mall or gym may be your best bet right now. Rest and take good care of yourself.

Losing a couple of pounds is definitely not worth a sun stroke!

118. Consider T'ai Chi for a fun exercise.

Several years ago my church had a T'ai Chi class. I have been seeing some people recently doing T'ai Chi in an advertisement for an arthritis medicine on television.

I have never been known for my graceful form. But when I took this class, I have never felt better physically and I actually felt poised and self-confident. This is such a beautiful, graceful, slow moving form of exercise.

I just ordered myself a new beginner tape and will try it again on my own. I can't find a class in my hometown.

If you haven't tried T'ai Chi… possibly it is just what you are looking for in an exercise program to add variety. (Check with your doctor before starting though…)

Humor

I think we always need a little humor in all that we do. I know losing weight is serious business, but a little levity never hurt. One of my readers a while back said, "Put speed bumps on the way to the refrigerator." And today a reader, Judy, said her favorite jokes were about weight loss. She shared this one...

A lady is terribly overweight, so her doctor puts her on a diet. "I want you to eat regularly for two days, then skip a day, and repeat this procedure for two weeks. The next time I see you, you'll have lost at least five pounds."

When the lady returns, she's lost nearly 20 pounds. "Why, that's amazing!" the doctor says. "Did you follow my instructions?"

The lady nods. "I'll tell you, though, I thought I was going to drop dead that third day."

"From hunger, you mean?"

"No, from skipping down the sidewalk." :-)

119. A pleasant 20 minute activity to easily burn off the calories in two cookies, ½ cup of pudding or ¼ cup of ice cream.

Did you know that you burn 100 calories by taking a brisk 20 minute walk (4 mph) around the neighborhood?

That's the same amount of calories in two cookies. 1/2 cup of pudding or a 1/4 cup of ice cream.

When you feel like splurging on dessert, just remember, that brisk walk will burn those calories off. And you won't feel guilty about having that special something.

120. A simple and practically effortless way to burn extra calories while you read, play, or watch television.

One of our readers, Agata said, "People who fidget (drum their fingers, tap their feet, etc.) have a higher metabolism on average than their more sedate counterparts."

I did a little checking and found that a recent Mayo Clinic study suggests that people who fidget burn hundreds of extra calories.

The people who gained the least weight were those who burned the most calories doing normal activities in their daily lives... i.e. fidgeting, moving around, and changing posture.

The good news of this study for those of us that aren't "fidgeters" is that every calorie you burn by moving around counts. So, increase your daily activities. Don't stay glued to your desk. Get up and walk around. MOVE!

I suppose when we tell our children to stop fidgeting--- maybe we shouldn't. Thanks Agata!

121. An easy way to lose weight and at the same time, give yourself a "second wind" after a tiring and stressful day at work.

I start my day with a brisk walk and then I go to an exercise group.

The camaraderie is great!!! We encourage each other. And we feel so much better after we leave.

However, sometimes topics come up that make me think about the tips I want to share with you.

One person said the reason Mary doesn't come is that she is too tired after work and she doesn't have time in the morning.

Believe it or not when you have a busy, stressful day you need a good brisk walk or a trip to the gym. It will give you a second wind and you will be better able to face the chores at home. **Find time for yourself**!!

Don't you think you are worth feeling great? When you add activity to your day, you can greet your family with a much better disposition. And you will rest so much better at night.

122. The formula for losing weight that never fails.

Energy In minus Energy Out =   The Key to losing weight

We put that **energy in** (food - calories.) But it is soooo hard sometimes to do the **energy out**... (physical activity.)

Did you know that it takes 3500 excess calories to gain a pound of fat? Then, your body has to use up those 3500 extra calories to lose that pound of fat.

This is why we think it sure was a lot easier to put those pounds on in the first place. We are enjoying that good food and we think, "One more order of French fries is not going to hurt." Hey... believe me... **it will**. Why not eat an apple instead?

Some where, and I'm not sure where I heard this: **"Nothing Tastes As Good As It Feels To Be Thin."** That's a "souper" heavy statement. You might think about that before you put that little something extra into your mouth.

123. Here are many ordinary exercise activities and how many calories you burn with each.

One of our readers, Le'ande, has asked that I share with you some exercises and the amount of calories they burn.

The Mayo Clinic gives us the following information as to approximate calories expended hourly by your weight.

Activity	150lb.	200lb.	250lb.
Bicycling 6mph	240	312	384
Bicycling 12 mph	410	534	660
Bowling	240	300	360
Calisthenics	300	360	420
Dancing	420	600	780
Jogging 7 mph	920	1230	1540
Jumping rope	750	1000	1250
Running in place	660	962	1264
Running 10 mph	1280	1664	2044
Swimming 25 yds/min	275	358	441
Swimming 50 yds/min	500	650	800
Tennis, singles	400	535	670
Walking, 2 mph	240	312	380
Walking 3 mph	320	416	600
Walking 4.5 mph	440	572	700

Walking is probably one of the best exercises to begin with. Start with 10 minutes and each week increase the length time you walk by 2 to 5 minutes. Keep adding increments until you can walk 45 minutes to an hour at a time.

As with any exercise or weight loss plan, please be sure to check with your doctor as to what is just right for you.

124. How you can burn calories and lose weight when doing simple activities such as talking on the phone and watching television... and others you wouldn't think of as calorie burning activities.

When talking on the telephone, take that wireless phone or cell phone and ride an exercise bike that is sitting in the corner gathering dust. Get up off that couch and turn the TV station instead of using that remote.

At work... take those stairs instead of the elevator. Park in the farthest parking space at work, the mall, or any where you go. If you are a golfer, walk that course instead of using the cart. Instead of going to a car wash (and if the weather permits) ....wash that car manually.

You will be very surprised at just how many hundreds of calories such small activities will burn over the course of a year... and how many pounds and inches you could remove!

125. How to determine how many calories any activity burns in an hour.

Another reader, Cari, asked me about how many calories you burn doing household chores like laundry, vacuuming, etc.

There is a web site at **Primus Web** http://primusweb.com/fitnesspartner/jumpsite/calculat.htm that lets you calculate the calories burned for doing all sorts of activities... from aerobics to watching TV and standing in line.

You simply enter your weight and length of time you perform the activity... and it gives you the number of calories burned for almost any activity you can imagine!

For instance, someone weighing 150 pounds doing heavy cleaning, washing a car or windows burns 162 calories in 30 minutes. A 175-pound person will burn 189 calories in 30 minutes. A 200-pound person would burn 216 for the same length.

I had to stand in line the other day for thirty minutes and I could even calculate this. Every activity we do burns calories. So let's keep moving!

126. Here are new ways to make your exercising activity more fun.

Make Your Activity/Exercise a fun time. Boredom is the death of any weight loss exercise program. Diversify your activities with dancing, swimming, bicycling, or gardening. Make it something you already love to do.

Sue, one of my readers, said she likes to listen to her radio while using her stationary bike and move her arms to the music. Afterwards she goes for a swim.

When I walk, I have a tape of marches that really gets me going. I played French horn in the band in high school, and I really like the extra "umph" marches give me during my walk. Hearing John Philip Sousa with his "Stars and Stripes" and other similar marches really makes my walk so much more enjoyable.

My friend, Betty, broke her leg about a year ago and has had to limit her walking. But, she is the gardener for her church. She can't do all the things she used to, but she bends and stoops and plants the most beautiful flowers.

Everything Betty touches seems to grow. I saw a sign the other day that said "Everything grows with love." She plants it with love... love for her church and love for what she is doing. She is staying fit and trim, and has fun doing it.

For activities to be successful, we have to make it something we love to do.

127. How to make exercising a super fun activity. Use these tips and your exercise program will never become a bore or a chore!

Our reader, Andrena from Glasgow, Scotland said, "If any of your readers are like me, I find going to the gym or jogging a very tedious and unpleasant experience, coupled with the fact that by the time I get home from work I am tired.

I used to go to the gym and only managed to keep it up for a few weeks. Now that I go swimming at lunchtime, I have found a space in my life when I can exercise at a point in the day when I have the energy. On top of that, swimming is fun and good for you. With any luck this will become a lifelong habit that helps me to stay in shape."

Some of our readers have found that sharing their exercise time with a favorite person like Jean and Jen do helps. As I told both of them, this type of exercise is doubly rewarding. You are spending quality time with someone you love... and reaping the benefits of exercise along with it.

"For exercise," Jean says, "I just take my 3-year-old granddaughter, Cheyenne, outside and I do everything she does as we play follow the leader or copycat or something. She loves it, and believe me, I get a workout! I am 52 and it's hard to do what a 3-year-old does for about an hour at a time! I get to spend quality playtime with Cheyenne and get my exercise at the same time."

Jen says, "My husband and I get up and go to the gym every morning before work at 5:45am. Its hard to crawl out of bed some mornings, but knowing how great I'll feel afterwards, and having my husband with me gives me that little boost I need to get up and going. On top of it all, it's a great energizer for the rest of the day."

As we've reminded you before, you have to love what you are doing or it will not last. You will not follow through for the long haul.

128. What music is best to listen to while walking?

Our readers Jen and Filomena like to work out to music like I do! Jen said, "One of the things that gets me motivated when I do my 30 minutes on the Stairmaster is Shania Twain. Her "Come on Over" tape (side 2) has a great beat through the whole thing and lasts the whole half hour. Its perfect."

Filomena adds, "I'm a classical music musician, but I love to walk to country music. It has such a good steady beat."

129. Use these simple low cost accessories to help you burn even more calories on your daily wａｉｎ

As an avid walker, I'm always looking for things to improve my weight loss efforts while walking. In an recent article about walking, "Weighted Vests" were mentioned.

I have used one pound hand weights and some weighted gloves, but am not familiar with the vest. Researchers at Oregon State University found that use of the weighted vest during exercise and walking, was not only helpful for losing weight... but also prevented bone loss in the hips of post menopausal women.

It's always great to have things that will be beneficial in more ways than one. Getting and/or staying slim and improving your bone density at the same time is a plus in any weight loss program.

However, this may be a walking accessory that we will need to reserve for the winter months. It looks as if it might be very warm for the summer.

Polly wrote, "I have not used the weighted vest but I did start walking with a weighted backpack. I put a ten pound weight in the pack and carry it low against the small of my back. On weekends I put in 15 pounds.

I had been losing about 1/2 pound a week prior to adding the weight. The last three consecutive weeks I have lost a pound (per week) and did not change anything else in my slimming routine. I assume the vest works in a similar fashion."

And from Jane, "Down Under"... "My daughter and I walk every morning (except, maybe Sundays). Three days per week, we walk 5 kilometers, and the other days, we do a fast 2 kilometer walk.

We vary the route so that we don't become used to the same thing. As we live in a slightly hilly area, we get lots of benefits, whichever way we choose to walk.

We are enjoying winter at the moment, and have to wear jackets whenever we venture outside. However, in the warmer months, we wear little cotton vests. They have pockets at waist level, and I fill them will heavy things.

Just taking your wallet, keys, and cell phone will add some weight (sadly, walking in the city, these items are necessities for safety these days), but if you put a couple of stones in too, you can increase the weight.

Though I agree that the weighted vests are a good idea, many people cannot afford to purchase specialty items. Simply adding a couple of smooth, clean stones in your pockets will achieve the same result."

130. Here's how to use your posture to trim your tummy and burn extra calories with little or no effort.

My mom used to say, "sit up straight! Don't slouch! Grow tall!" Mom's are always right!

My grown-up daughter is relatively tall. She was once asked in a survey what was the most important advice her mother ever gave her. Her answer was, "Stand up straight, keep your chest out, and look like you're proud of yourself!"

Did you know that simply by standing up straight you look slimmer and trimmer?

Along those same lines is an article in First (for Women) Magazine about keeping your eyes up instead of looking at the ground when you are walking or jogging.

It seems that even the slightest slump keeps your diaphragm and lungs from filling up easily. But, if you watch your posture and stand up straight while walking or jogging, you will have more energy for taking an extra step... and burning extra calories.

So whether standing, walking, or sitting, stand tall! Lots of good benefits.

Did you know that standing up tall and not slumping will also help you to burn calories?

Dr. Barbara Rolls, food-nutrition researcher at Pennsylvania State University says that good posture will help to strengthen your abdominal muscles and helps to slim your stomach!

131. Little things mean a lot when you eat them... check this out!

So many times we rationalize our eating. We think those little extras are not going to effect our weight loss efforts. You know... a few fries at the local hamburger place, an extra packet of dressing at dinner, a jelly donut on coffee break...

But did you know that you have to walk the following lengths of time at a pace of 3 mph to burn up these extra calories?

Large Fries - 72 minutes 8 Onion Rings - 35 minutes Hash Browns, Half cup - 30 minutes Garlic Bread, 1 Slice - 22 minutes Ranch Dressing, 1 pack - 46 minutes Jelly Doughnut - 45 minutes

All these times are approximate and are based on a 150 pound woman. But when you think what you have to do to get rid these calories, it sure puts things in a different light. The next time you reach for that extra something... think of what you will have to do to get rid of it.

Chapter Eight

Lagniappe Secrets
**(As the Louisiana Cajun people say,
"A little bit extra for good measure.")**

132. How adjusting the temperature of your bedroom can help you lose weight!

Here's a tip from Dr. Barbara Rolls, who is a food-nutrition researcher at Pennsylvania State University. "If you keep your bedroom chilly at night you will naturally burn more calories."

133. Why ordinarily good-for-you cabbage or other green leafy veggies could be a "natural" killer if you're on certain medications!

One of our readers, Ramona, asked me to remind you that before starting the Souper Soup Weight Loss Plan or any weight loss plan for that matter, you should check with your doctor.

If you will notice... the very first thing we tell you when you receive the Souper Soup recipe is a statement reminding you to check with your doctor first before starting any weight loss plan.

This is most important for everyone, but it is especially so if you have a medical condition such as heart problems, high blood pressure, diabetes, etc.

Ramona said, "**Be careful with cabbage and/or any green leafy vegetables if you are taking any kind of blood thinners such as coumadin or warfarin for heart disease**. These vegetables are full of vitamin K and potassium which can render your blood thinner useless and lead to a heart attack."

Getting a professional opinion first is also important when starting any new exercise program. To avoid injury, please check with your family doctor just to be on the safe side.

134. Here is a simple but pleasurable little item available everywhere for only pennies that will increase your metabolic rate by 20% and take off 10 pounds with absolutely no effort.

Another one of the great tips I received from a reader is chewing gum. Beverly says, "Chewing gum gives your mouth something to do, gives you flavor without calories, and keeps the saliva going to your stomach so you don't get as hungry."

We still need a pacifier sometimes and gum makes a good one. Be sure you get the sugar-free kind.

Also, the Mayo Clinic reports that chewing sugarless gum boosted metabolism by 20 per cent. At that rate, you could lose a possible 10 pounds in a year simply from chewing gum regularly!

135. Use "The Dieter's Prayer" to keep from denying yourself some of the things you really like.

The Dieter's Prayer: God grant me the serenity to accept the things I ought to eat, the courage to avoid the things I shouldn't eat, and the wisdom to know that a little chocolate never hurt anyone!

Within reason--- don't completely eliminate the one thing you especially like when you are planning your weight loss program.

I really like having **real** salad dressing. I would rather have a little bit of the real thing than lots of the low calorie kind.

And, you do need some fat in your diet. Build a good salad with lots of good veggies, some grated soy cheese, and have a serving of your favorite dressing.

Don't deny yourself of some things you really like.

136. Here are low cost gadgets available at Walmart that will make your life easier and help you lose weight.

I can't pass a gadget counter at my favorite department store without wanting to go in and look for something else to make food preparation quicker and easier. When you are trying to lose weight, cooking should be an easy, fun thing to do.

There are wonderful rice cookers, veggie steamers, or something as simple as some good knives. The knives will help with chopping the fruits and veggies you prepare ahead of time to avoid the wrong kind of snacking.

One of my favorite "new gadgets" that I recently purchased was one of the new, small ice cream makers. There are delicious recipes for low fat and sugar free ice creams and yogurts that come with it. I have found that fresh or frozen peaches really add a lot to the "home made" ice cream flavor. I used some fresh ones that I had frozen.

A garlic press is another good item to use in your creative menus. And, one of my favorite items in the kitchen is my George Foreman Grill. It makes for such a great way to cook delicious low-fat meals. So when you are tempted the next time at the mall to check out the house wares department, do check out some of these items.

Buying a helpful gadget is also a good way to reward yourself without eating food.

137. Tricks to help you lose weight if you live and/or eat alone.

There is an old saying that you should treat family like company and your company like family.

Get out your china and silverware and surprise your family. What are you saving it for anyway? Put some fresh flowers on the table. Try a new recipe and don't tell the family that it is low calorie. Make eating a special occasion. Sit down and enjoy the meal as if it were an extraordinary event. Talk to your family.

So--- you live by yourself. I did for a long time too. And I found that if I put on a special place mat or table cloth, and served my meal on a pretty dish--- It was easier to sit down and not inhale my food.

Make your food look inviting. Dress it up. Put the flowers or decorations on your table just as if you were expecting special company.

You are special!

138. Do you have a spouse or child who needs to lose some weight but won't commit to the effort? Here are some little "deceptive cooking" tricks to help them and they'll never notice the difference from your "regular cooking."

One of my readers recently wrote for help with a friend who wants to lose weight but won't commit to it. This is very frustrating to the "COOK." Following is what I told them.

If you have someone who needs to lose pounds, or just plain eat healthier, get out your favorite recipes and cut the fat and sugar in them.

But don't tell the person what you're doing.

There are many low calorie, low fat items you can use in your cooking. Read labels. Get out the "Pam" instead of the cooking oil. Use apple sauce in your cakes instead of oil. Drain any excess oil from things like bacon or sausage on paper towels. Wash the fat off of oil packed tuna.

Make your food as appealing and tasty as possible. Herbs add a lot to recipes. Be creative. Believe me, I cook low fat for my family all the time and they don't even know it. No complaints.

Cutting calories any way you can will help in your weight loss efforts.

I once knew someone who did this with her husband. When he was able to get into some pants he hadn't worn for a while, he said to her, "Dear, I believe something is wrong with me I am losing weight!" She had to confess up then.

Try a little "deception" with your cooking now and then. It will be good for all.

139. How Lillie's "takes one to know one" weight loss problems can help you lose the weight you want to lose.

Several tips recipients have emailed me... wondering if I was a "skinny minnie" who never had to worry about my own weight. Since you can't see me, it seems the image of me is that of a very thin person who had never had a weight problem in her life.

Not so. Believe me, I have the same weight problems as you!

There was a time in my life when I was very skinny. But like most girls--- when we have children the weight comes on and it is not so easy to come off. I have been fighting this battle for a long time. And, I still have to watch what I eat every day.

This is a lifetime commitment to healthy eating. This is not to say that I do not over eat and enjoy the foods I like to eat on occasion, but I know I can't do this routinely.

I feel so much better since I have taken this approach to my life. I look better in my clothes and I am very active!

Just thought you'd like to know.

140. How wearing the right clothing can give a boost to your weight loss efforts.

What can I wear to that special holiday party?

Check out your closet and see if your clothes are too big. Clothing that is too big for you makes you look larger than you really are!

Get rid of those big clothes. Sell them at a resale shop and while there, see if there are party clothes you can buy for a small amount. You don't want to invest a large amount in clothes if you are still losing weight.

Buying one good fitting item can do wonders for your self-esteem. Looking good, watching your posture and feeling good about yourself in general can make you really shine at those parties---. People will notice that there is something different about you. You'll feel so good when you're asked, "Have you lost weight?"

Make sure your clothes fit. Clothes that hug the figure show every flaw. Also-- big, baggy clothes make you look a couple of sizes larger. (We don't need that!)

Fabrics, also, should be considered in choosing your clothes. Fabrics such as tweed, velvet, or bulky knits with a heavy feel can pile on the look of extra pounds. Natural fabrics, such as cotton, silk and linen are always excellent choices.

141. How your cat or dog can help you lose weight.

Not only do I have trouble with my weight from time to time, but my dog does also.

Like so many other well meaning friends and family members of mine, I tend to be a "feeder."

When the vet put my mutt on a diet, I thought of how I could apply this to my own weight related problems.

First, he and I are going for walks. We both benefit.

Second, his treats are limited. Likewise, I am limiting mine.

Third, think how it feels when someone is pushing food on you, even when you know you don't need it.

So if you are as fortunate to have a "pet friend" include them in your diet program and you will both benefit.

142. How choosing the size of your plate can help you lose weight.

Two of our readers suggested the use of smaller plates to help control the amount eaten.

Beverly said she used the small plates that come with your sets of dishes that no one uses, such as dessert plates. She said, " Even if you pile them high, you can't get too much in it."

Angie also suggested using smaller plates. She added that you don't have to finish everything on your plate.

Our mothers encouraged us to clean our plates with a giant guilt trip about "those starving children." I never could understand how that helped them, but I cleaned my plate. And it is easy to fall back into this pattern as adults.

Those leftovers don't help anyone and they certainly add calories for you.

Along the same line of eating in smaller amounts, you might try using my tip about getting or putting your salad dressing on the side and dipping only your fork in it before each bite of salad. This limits your intake greatly.

Think smaller amounts!

143. Here's how to make losing weight a fun thing to do.

It gets to be serious.... this business of losing weight and keeping it off. But as with all serious things we need a little levity.

Sometimes we get too caught up with how much we are losing and how quickly. We want it to be faster. We want it to happen all at once.

We have a lot more fun putting on weight than taking it off!

Try having some fun in your weight loss efforts. Don't take yourself so seriously. Don't eat the same thing all the time. Try some new recipes.

Start a new hobby... one that will keep you away from that refrigerator. Make time for yourself. It is so important!

144. How reducing your sodium intake can help reduce your weight as well as your blood pressure.

Reducing your sodium intake is a great factor in losing weight. According to Mayo Clinic, when your body builds up excess fat it tends to retain sodium. This can lead to high-blood pressure. Decreasing your weight and sodium intake lowers your blood pressure.

One of my pet peeves is for someone to come in my home for dinner and start salting their meal before they have even tasted it. This to me is very rude, not to mention they may have just over salted what they are about to eat. Nothing tastes worse than food that is too salty, plus it is not healthy.

When dining out, check your menu for items that are in cocktail sauce. Also, beware of the terms pickled, smoked, teriyaki, or au jus when they appear on the menu. Many restaurants use high-sodium, meat-based products for sauces. You can request that your foods be prepared without MSG (monosodium glutamate.) Request soy sauce (which is high in sodium) on the side.

Another source in which to watch your sodium is canned veggies. Salt is often used in the canning process. Be sure to look for cans with "no salt added" or rinse your veggies in a colander before preparing. Fresh veggies are naturally low in sodium.

145. Here's how the route you take through a supermarket can help you lose weight.

"Shopping On The Edge"

In the United States we tend to take a lot of things for granted. In researching new information for you, we stumbled onto something. This was just so very obvious that I thought, "Wow... why haven't I noticed this before?

The next time you take a trip to your local grocery store... notice the arrangement or layout of it.

I have been to all the supermarkets in my area and in neighboring areas. They ALL have the same general layout. Do you know that you can shop the perimeter of your grocery and not even make the middle aisles... and buy every kind of healthy food that you need?

All the supermarkets in my area start with produce, fruits and veggies, which also has a juice refrigerator. Next is bread, followed by seafood, then fresh meats, and poultry. Then comes the dairy... milk, eggs, cheese. Wow! What a revelation.

I don't even have to go near those aisles with temptations galore to prepare a healthy meal. I even noticed that coffee and tea are near the end of an aisle, so again I didn't have to take a trip down them. Also the cereals such as oatmeal, rice, etc. are also located at the ends.

To avoid temptation... make that grocery list and try "shopping on the edge." Leave your cart at the end of the counter and walk down the aisle to pick up what you must have. You will not be as tempted to pick up more than you need.

146. Shopping secrets to help you lose weight while saving you money.

Three of the most important things to remember when shopping is read labels, read labels, and read labels.

I can't stress enough how important it is to READ labels. There are so many misleading claims when it comes to "lite" foods. And "fat free" foods can be the biggest culprit of them all.

Fat is one of the things in food that makes them taste so good. I am from the south and my mother used to save bacon drippings to put in her fresh veggies. They were wonderful. But after a night in the frig you could skim off a quarter inch of fat.

So to make up for the wonderful taste of "fat"... sugar is now substituted in a lot of the products on the market. Also, watch the sodium content. Salt too is a flavor enhancer.

When shopping, don't be in a hurry. Make sure that what goes into your buggy is truly low fat **and** low calorie.

And remember my tip about shopping on the edge of the store. The healthier foods are always found around the edge of the store.

147. Here's how you can go on vacation without blowing your weight loss plan

When you plan for your vacation, don't take a vacation from your weight loss efforts.

With some planning you can choose to stay the same weight or even lose weight while on vacation. If you have lost pounds to fit into a swim suit or special vacation clothes, don't blow it by taking a vacation from your weight loss plan.

There a few simple things that you can do to make your weight loss efforts as successful away from home as they were at home.

(1.) Plan your "eating" day. If you are going out for dinner choose a light breakfast and lunch. Save the bulk of your calories for the evening meal.

(2.) If you are a dessert lover like me, choose something like grilled chicken or fish for your entree' and share that dessert with a friend. Choose lots of fruits and veggies.

(3.) Get in as much activity as possible. Walk to restaurants that are close to your hotel. Find out what your hotel has to offer in the way of fitness equipment and take advantage of it. You are paying for it you know. Walk everywhere you can.

(4) If a road trip, be sure to pack healthy snacks to eat along the way. Instead of soft drinks, carry lots of bottled water. (Be sure to get the sodium free type.)

(5) And if you feel that, just maybe, you have enjoyed yourself a little too much on the trip, DON'T beat yourself up. Get back to your weight loss program as soon as possible when you get back home.

Make it a guilt-free vacation!

148. Can you lose weight while you sleep? This one is going to really surprise you!

You've seen the ads promising such. Most of us don't believe this promise... but listen to this!

A new research program just reported by the prestigious JAMA (Journal of American Medical Association) shows that loss of sleep definitely interferes with weight loss!

According to the report, sleep loss is associated with the hormones which regulate appetite. Lack of sleep also affects our metabolism in a way to keep from burning off fat even though we are eating healthy and exercising.

The report says that eight hours of sleep each night is recommended for adults, but studies show less than one-third of adults get that much sleep... especially on week nights.

JAMA's recommendations for getting eight hours of sleep include:

1. Don't go to bed hungry - but avoid eating right before bed time.

2. Exercise regularly... but do so at least three hours before bed time.

3. Establish good sleep habits by going to bed and getting up at the same time every day.

149. How to use Apple Cider Vinegar to melt fat off your body like fire melts ice... while you eat three meals a day of delicious wholesome food... including desserts!

One of the most powerful appetite suppressants we know is Apple Cider Vinegar. Mix a tablespoon of vinegar with a teaspoon of honey in a glass of water. Drink this ½ hour before you sit down to eat every meal. This works better than any diet pill you can buy anywhere... and is oh so much better for you!

Emily Thacker has written a great book on using Apple Cider Vinegar to lose weight. It is an international best seller with over three million copies in print! You can take a look at it at http://lillieross.com/vindiet1.htm

Continue Your Weight Loss Success

You now have the ammunition you need to lose weight and keep it off without being deprived, going hungry or using diet pills.

At this point you should consider a long term personal weight loss advisor as well as a personal support group. Both are **yours free** as a benefit of buying this book.

First, make sure you are connected to the internet and go to **Daily Weight Loss Tips** at **http://www.lillieross.com/freetips.htm** Simply scroll to the bottom of the page, then enter your first name and your email address.

This will put you on the list to start receiving *Lillie's Daily Weight Loss Tip*. Each morning, Tuesday through Friday you will receive in your email, a short, concise tip such as the ones we've included in this book under "Lillie's Secrets." You can easily unsubscribe at any time you like.

We spend thousands of dollars subscribing to the research letters of major universities and research labs world-wide and bring you the best of all of them. Anytime there is a breakthrough in weight loss science, as a Daily Weight Loss Tip subscriber, you will be among the first to know!

Next, you will want to be connected to the internet then click on **"Lillie's Weight Loss Support Group"** at http://www.lillieross.com/support.htm and take a look. Even if you don't have an immediate problem, you will enjoy reading the posted messages and can possibly help someone else.

Enjoy!

Here's to slimming down and feeling great!

Lillie Ross
lillie@lillieross.com

Chapter Nine

Low Calorie – Low Fat Soup Recipes

Simply can't stand the taste of our Souper Soup? Or… maybe you need a break for the same taste before every meal?

Here are delicious pinch-hitters. Have a hot steaming bowl of one of these creations before each of your meals. Then, watch the pounds and inches fall away!

Tomato Eggplant Soup
Makes 8 servings

2 – 10.5 oz. cans condensed tomato soup
2 medium eggplants
½ cup chicken broth

Cook eggplants at 350 degrees F (175 degrees C) for 30-40 minutes until soft. Scoop out insides and puree eggplant. Stir tomato soup and pureed eggplant together and bring to a boil. Simmer for 5 minutes and add chicken broth to thin soup to taste.

Nutrition per serving
90 calories
3g protein
1.5g total fat
474mg sodium
0mg cholesterol
18.5g carbohydrates
3.7g fiber

Chicken Soup
Makes 16 servings

2 tablespoons vegetable oil
2 chicken legs and thighs, skinned
1/2 cup chopped onion
2 quarts water
3 cubes chicken bouillon, crumbled
    1 stalk celery, chopped
3 carrots, chopped
1 clove roasted garlic, minced
salt and pepper to taste
1 (12 ounce) package thin egg noodles

In a large pot over medium heat, cook chicken pieces in oil until browned on both sides. Stir in onion and cook 2 minutes more. Pour in water and chicken bouillon and bring to a boil. Reduce heat and simmer 45 minutes.

Stir in celery, carrots, garlic, salt and pepper. Simmer until carrots are just tender. Remove chicken pieces and pull the meat from the bone. Stir the noodles into the pot and cook until tender, 10 minutes. Return chicken meat to pot just before serving.

Nutrition per serving:
113 calories
5.1g protein
3.5g total fat
239mg sodium
25mg cholesterol
15.1g carbohydrates
1.1g fiber

French Tomato Soup
Makes 6 servings

1 tablespoon butter
1 large onion, chopped
6 tomatoes, peeled and quartered

1 large potato, peeled and quartered
6 cups water
1 bay leaf
1 clove garlic, pressed
1 teaspoon salt
1/2 cup long-grain rice

Melt butter in a large saucepan over medium heat. Saute onions in butter until tender and lightly browned, about 10 minutes. Add tomatoes, and continue cooking for 10 more minutes, stirring frequently.

Add the potato, and 2 cups of water. Season with the bay leaf, garlic and salt. Bring to a boil, then reduce heat and simmer covered for about 20 minutes.

Stir in the remaining water, and bring to a boil again. Discard bay leaf, and strain the solids from the broth, reserving both.

Puree the vegetables in a food processor or blender, and stir them back into the broth. Bring to a boil, and add the rice.

Cover and simmer over low heat for about 15 minutes, or until rice is tender.

Serve hot with toasted French bread topped with melted low fat Swiss cheese.

Nutrition per serving:
134 calories
3.1g protein
2.5g total fat
429mg sodium
5mg Cholesterol
2.8g fiber

Fat-Free Vegetable Soup
Makes 12 servings

14 cups water
2 onions, chopped
2 large carrots, sliced
2 potatoes, peeled and cubed
2 green bell peppers, diced
1 (28 ounce) can whole peeled
   tomatoes with liquid, mashed
1 tablespoon chicken bouillon powder
1/4 teaspoon ground black pepper
2 teaspoons curry powder (optional)
3 cups finely shredded cabbage
2 stalks celery, chopped
1 1/2 cups cauliflower florets
3 teaspoons dried dill weed

In a large cooking pot, measure water, add onions, carrots, potatoes, green peppers, mashed tomatoes, chicken soup base, black pepper, and curry powder. Boil for 20 minutes or until carrots are tender.

Add shredded cabbage, chopped celery, cauliflower florets, and dill weed, then cook an additional 10 to 15 minutes. If soup is too thick, add more water and bring to boil. Season to taste.

Nutrition per serving
59 calories
2.4g protein
0.4g total fat
304mg sodium
1mg cholesterol
13g carbohydrates
3.2g fiber

Quick and Easy Vegetable Soup
Makes 6 servings

1 (14 ounce) can chicken broth
1 (11.5 ounce) can
  tomato-vegetable juice cocktail
1 cup water
1 large potato, diced
2 carrots, sliced
2 stalks celery, diced
1 (14.5 ounce) can diced tomatoes
1 cup chopped fresh green beans
1 cup fresh whole kernel corn
salt and pepper to taste
Creole seasoning to taste

In a large stock pot, combine broth, tomato juice, water, potatoes, carrots, celery, undrained chopped tomatoes, green beans, and corn.

Season with salt, pepper and Cajun/Creole seasoning. Bring to a boil and simmer for 30 minutes or until all vegetables are tender.

Nutrition per serving:
97 calories
3.5g protein
0.9g total fat
629mg sodium
0mg cholesterol
19.4g carbohydrates
3.9g fiber

Low-Fat Broccoli Soup
Makes 6 servings

2 cups water
3/4 cups celery; chopped
1 tb olive oil
2 tb flour

3/4 ts salt
1/8 ts nutmeg
1 1/2 lb broccoli; stalks separated
1/2 cup onion; chopped
2 1/2 cups water
1 tb instant chicken bouillon
1/8 ts pepper
1/2 cup evaporated skim milk

Heat 2 cups water in a large pot until boiling. Add vegetables, cover, and cook until tender (about 10 min)

Blend vegetables with part of the cooking water in a blender or food processor.

Heat olive oil in a small nonstick skillet. Add 2 T of the 2 1/2 cups water and sprinkle in the flour. Cook and stir until smooth.

Add the remaining water and heat to boiling, stirring constantly. Boil and stir for one minute.

Stir broccoli mixture, instant bouillon, salt, pepper, and nutmeg. Heat until boiling.

Stir in the evaporated skim milk and heat through without boiling again.

Nutrition per 1 1/2 cup serving:
86 calories
1mg. cholesterol
5g fiber
3g fat
371mg sodium.

Okra Gumbo Soup
Makes 8 servings

1 tablespoon vegetable oil
1 clove garlic, minced

1 medium onion, finely chopped
1 medium green bell pepper finely chopped
1/2 (16 ounce) package frozen okra, thawed and sliced
8 ounces fresh mushrooms, sliced
1 (14.5 ounce) can diced tomatoes with juice
1 (6 ounce) can tomato paste
1/2 teaspoon file powder
2 bay leaves
1 teaspoon salt
1 teaspoon ground black pepper
2 tablespoons vegetable oil
2 tablespoons all-purpose flour

Heat 1 tablespoon oil in a large saucepan over medium heat. Stir in garlic, onion, and green bell pepper, and saute until tender. Stir in okra, mushrooms, diced tomatoes and their liquid, tomato paste, file powder, bay leaves, salt, and pepper. Cook, stirring occasionally, 40 minutes.

Heat 2 tablespoons oil in a medium skillet over medium heat. Stirring constantly, add flour, and cook 2 to 5 minutes, until a golden brown roux has formed.

Spoon the roux into the okra mixture, and continue to cook, stirring occasionally, 5 to 10 minutes, until thickened.

"File" powder (pronounced "fil-a" is a seasoning made from the ground, dried leaves of the sassafras tree. It's an integral part of Cajun and Creole cooking. It is used to thicken and flavor Gumbos and other Cajun or Creole dishes.

Nutrition per serving
107 calories
3g protein
5.5g total fat
541mg sodium
0mg cholesterol
12.8g carbohydrates, 2.9g fiber

Low-Fat Ham & Bean Soup
Makes 5 servings

1 cup sliced green onion
1 cup diced celery
1 large clove garlic, minced
1/2 tsp. dried thyme leaves
4 cups low-sodium chicken broth
3 cups water
1 can (15oz.) cooked cannellini beans (white kidney beans)
or navy beans
2 ozs. uncooked elbow macaroni
1/2 lb. lean ham, diced
1/8 tsp. freshly ground pepper
1/4 cup chopped fresh parsley
2-3 drops hot red pepper sauce

In a large saucepan sprayed with nonstick spray, stir-fry green onion, celery, garlic and thyme over medium-high heat for 2-3 minutes, until tender.

Add broth and water. Bring to a boil.

Meanwhile, puree half the beans at a time in a blender or food processor.

Add macaroni, ham, pepper, parsley, hot pepper sauce and beans to boiling soup stock. Simmer covered, for 30 minutes.

(nutrition values not available)

Here's A Physician With The Right "Prescription" For Losing Weight!

Let Dr. Joy Siegrist, MD show you a safe, easy way to lose weight. Quickly and easily Get to... and stay at... your ideal weight.

You can download it right now and start losing weight today! You'll lose weight faster than if you jogged 6 miles every day! Measure the difference in your waist-line faster than any other program... and you won't gain it back.

13 year medically proven... 96% success rate! No pills, no drugs, no shakes, no diet-patches, no meal replacements, no side-effects, and it's great for diabetics.

Dr. Siegrist's program has been successful for thousands who never thought they could lose weight and keep it off without starving.

Now it's your turn.

Visit: http://www.lillieross.com/drsiegrist.htm
right now to check out her program and success photos.

Your Life Just Got A Little Sweeter! Here's how you can actually eat TWO portions of your favorite dessert and still lose weight

Trying to give up sweets is the downfall of many a dieter. With this secret, you not only do **not** have to give up your favorite dessert... but you can even have two portions if you are particularly "sweet hungry" some days. Here's how:

If you want to lose weight and keep it off... and/or if you cook for a diabetic... you simply **must** consider this!

Splenda is a relatively new... amazing substitute for sugar. Now, for the first time, you can cook and bake with little or no sugar and produce delicious, sweet, super satisfying treats.

Now, culinary nutritionist Marlene Koch shows you over 80 mouth-watering desserts you can prepare in your own kitchen... low calorie, low fat, and either no-sugar or little-sugar.

We talking about scrumptious Cakes, Pies, Smoothies, Cookies, Muffins, Drinks, Cheesecakes, Creampuffs, and many more!

These are not pale imitations, but delectable desserts and beverages that look good and taste so incredibly good that you simply won't believe they aren't full of sugar, fat, or calories.

Even with **big** "real size" portions, all these desserts are 200 calories or less... most in the 100 to 160 calorie range. Visit http://www.lillieross.com/splenda2.htm to take a look **now**!

"Gracious Dining
With America's First - First Lady"

With hundreds of servants at her command... a person would think our first First Lady was a woman of leisure.

Far from it, according to a new historical discovery. A long out-of-print volume entitled, "The Martha Washington Cook Book" reveals that Mrs. Washington personally supervised her entire household staff... and especially the kitchen and dining room servants.

Even more amazing than the delicious recipes cooked up in the Washington kitchen... you'll really be astonished to learn who sat at the head of the table and who carved the meat at the Washington dining table.

Visit the web site below to find out right now!
http://www.lillieross.com/martha.htm

"Uncommon Uses for Common Household Products"

Remove a broken lightbulb from the socket with a potato!

Clean leather coats and handbags with cold cream.

Keep your computer and TV screen dust free with this common item from your laundry room!

Why spend money on expensive cleaners, wax removers, fertilizers, wood stain and insecticides... when shaving cream, tea, hot sauce and dish soap work just as well at a small fraction of the cost.

Visit the web site:
http://www.lillieross.com/tips.htm
for scads of FREE Incredibly Ingenious Tips and Other Offbeat Uses For Household Products!

Vinegar Can Be Used For What?

A Teaspoon A Day Helps Keep The Doctor Away!

A daily teaspoon of vinegar, nature's powerful healing food, seems to remedy many ills of the world.

Now 308 of the worlds best healing & cleaning remedies are packed into "The Vinegar Book."

You'll use vinegar to soothe arthritis, joint pains, sore throats, fade age spots, shed pounds, remedy infections, cool sunburns, remove corns & calluses, dandruff, diarrhea, ear-toothaches AND hundreds more. Plus, countless cleaning agents.

Take a look at it now at:
http://www.lillieross.com/vinegar2.htm

Discover Why Folks From the Old South Seemed to Live Forever and Never Lose the Glow of Youth!

Now, famed researcher Emily Thacker has put together the most comprehensive collection ever of "Home Remedies from the Old South." Most of these amazing remedies can be made with just one or two common ingredients found in your kitchen cabinet or refrigerator.

Learn how you can lose weight, look better, feel better... or quickly and easily relieve pain.

Visit the website at:
http://www.lillieross.com/oldsouth.htm
to take a free look!

Are You Over 55...
or have a loved one who is?
"It's All Free For Seniors"

It's incredible what you can get free when you know where to ask!

This amazing new report reveals thousands of little-known Government give-aways for people over 55. There are details about getting free prescription drugs, dental care, legal help---, free money to remodel your home, how to get aid to travel--- and much, much more.

Many of these fabulous freebies can be yours regardless of your income or assets.

Click On: http://www.lillieross.com/free.htm
to see how this can work for you!

Suzanne Somers

You've seen the beautiful, vivacious, slim and trim Miss Suzanne Somers on many television programs as well as in the movies.

Ms. Somers has not always been slim and trim, however. At one time she found herself far overweight. This, of course, can quickly spell unemployment for an actress.

Suzanne called in a team of the best doctors and trainers in the U.S.A. to help her develop a program to quickly and easily get rid of her excess weight.

Since then, she has helped literally millions use her Somersize program to lose weight without hunger, pills, or extensive exercise. Several of her weight loss books have stayed at the top of the New York Times best seller lists for months at a time.

Suzanne's best program by far is her video set. It not only tells you how to lose weight, but actually SHOWS you how. We have difficulty keeping it in stock.
Visit the link below and take a look at what the Suzanne Somers Somersize program can do for you!
http://www.lillieross.com/suzanne4.htm

"Here's How You Can
Get Skinny While Eating Fabulous Food!"

Find out why "Somersizing" has swept the nation! In "Get Skinny on Fabulous Food," (a number one New York Times bestseller) Suzanne Somers will show you how to shed pounds for good and have more energy than ever before... without dieting.

Here is Suzanne's updated weight loss program that has helped over 2 million people lose weight while eating the foods they love. With over 100 new recipes, you and your family will be amazed that you can eat like this and still lose weight!

Visit the website below right now to take a look!
http://www.lillieross.com/suzanne2.htm